D1614287

AMERICAN INDIAN NOVELISTS

GARLAND REFERENCE LIBRARY
OF THE HUMANITIES
(VOL. 384)

AMERICAN INDIAN NOVELISTS
An Annotated Critical Bibliography

Tom Colonnese
Louis Owens

GARLAND PUBLISHING, INC. · NEW YORK & LONDON
1985

Library of Congress Cataloging in Publication Data

Colonnese, Tom, 1950–
American indian novelists.

(Garland reference library of the humanities ; vol.
384)
Includes index.
1. American fiction—Indian authors—Bibliography.
2. American literature—Indian authors—Bio-bibliography.
3. Authors, Indian—20th century—Biography.   I. Owens,
Louis,   II. Title.   III. Series: Garland reference
library of the humanities ; v. 384.
Z1229.I52C65   1985   016.813′009′897   82-49135
[PS153.I52]
ISBN 0-8240-9199-X (alk. paper)

Printed on acid-free, 250-year-life paper
Manufactured in the United States of America

For Elizabeth and Kristin

CONTENTS

Preface

As nearly everyone is aware, "Indian" is difficult to define. N. Scott Momaday, Pulitzer Prize
winner and the best known Indian novelist today,
suggests that Indian is "an idea which a given man has
of himself." Momaday adds, "And it is a moral idea .
. . ." In this bibliography, we have attempted to
include all novelists who share in common the quality
of both considering themselves and being considered by
their communities as American Indian by heritage.
This category is admittedly broad and includes authors
who may be controversial, such as Jamake Highwater,
and authors who may be officially as little as one-
sixteenth Indian, as in the cases of Hyemeyohsts Storm
and John W. Tebbel, as well as full-bloods such as
Simon Pokagon, James Welch, and others. It includes
authors who write almost exclusively about what it
means to be Indian in America, such as Momaday, Leslie
Marmon Silko, and Welch among others, and it includes
authors who appear, in their novels at least, to be
very little concerned with their Indian heritage, such
as John Milton Oskison and Tebbel.

We have attempted to include here every novelist
who fits the above description, omitting a few whose
inclusion might be strongly questionable. In this
latter category fall such writers as John Rollin
Ridge, the Cherokee author whose book *The Life and
Adventures of Joaquin Murieta, the Celebrated California Bandit* may be so heavily fictionalized as to
approach the definition of novel but still remains too
much in the realm of biography for this bibliography.
Similarly, we have omitted Frank Waters, who may in-
deed have been part American Indian by heritage but
who always identified himself exclusively with his
white ancestry.

This selected bibliography is intended as an aid
to students of the American Indian novel and as a
guide to the rapidly expanding volume of critical
material dealing with Indian novelists. Although our
major focus is on the novels and their criticism, we
have also included a broad selection of each author's
shorter works, such as poems and short fiction appear-

ing in anthologies, articles and essays, interviews, and reviews. We have not attempted to be exhaustive in dealing with shorter publications, but to provide a very broad sampling; for example, when dealing with such a writer as John W. Tebbel, author of more than a hundred books and five hundred articles under his own name and as a ghost writer, a comprehensive listing would have been beyond the scope or purpose of the present work. Because of our focus on the American Indian novel, we have provided full annotation only for novels and for criticism dealing with those novels. And because only a few comprehensive studies or surveys of the Indian novel exist thus far, the reader will find here extensive references to these few, to studies such as Charles Larson's *American Indian Fiction*, Kenneth Rosen's "American Indian Literature: Current Condition and Suggested Research," Alan Velie's *Four American Indian Literary Masters*, and Kenneth Lincoln's *American Indian Renaissance*.

The authors are arranged alphabetically, with brief biographical sketch and primary and secondary sources for each. Primary novels and booklength publications are arranged chronologically in order of appearance, while shorter works are arranged alphabetically.

Acknowledgment and many thanks must go to those who helped make this bibliography possible: Misha Schutt, Virginia Elwood and the staff of Oviett Library at California State University Northridge; the CSUN and NAU English Departments who provided both support and research time; the Oklahoma State Historical Society, for their prompt and valuable assistance; and Louella Holter who translated our scribblings and fed them into the word processor. Finally much admiration and recognition must be shown to those who have produced such outstanding bibliographic work in this area previously, individuals such as Arlene Hirschfelder, Daniel Littlefield, Jr. and James W. Parins, and David H. Brumble.

Introduction

Although the first novel by an American Indian may be dated 1899, when Simon Pokagon published his *O-gî-mäw-kwē Mit-i-gwä-kî (Queen of the Woods)*, and although a few novels such as those of John Milton Oskison, John Joseph Mathews, and D'Arcy McNickle appeared in the 1920's and 1930's, a spectacular renaissance in American Indian fiction began only in 1968 with the publication of N. Scott Momaday's *House Made of Dawn*. When Momaday won the Pulitzer Prize for that novel in 1969, serious critical attention focused for the first time on a novel by an American Indian author. And as if Momaday had triggered a long-dormant need among Indian writers, the decade following *House Made of Dawn* saw the publication of a stunning number of novels by American Indian authors including Hyemyohsts Storm, Janet Campbell Hale, Nasnaga (Roger Russell), Chief George Pierre, Dallas Chief Eagle, Denton R. Bedford, Jamake Highwater, James Welch, Virginia Driving Hawk Sneve, Gerald Vizenor, and Leslie Silko. McNickle, Sneve, Highwater, and Hale have each contributed impressive works to the field of juvenile or young-adult fiction, and in 1970 the first novel by an Eskimo writer appeared when Markoosie's starkly naturalistic and powerful *Harpoon of the Hunter* was published in Canada. More recently, James Tucker and Paula Gunn Allen have added novels to the growing list of works by American Indian writers.

In the works included here, one can easily trace the coming-of-age of the American Indian novel. Beginning with Pokagon's heavily romantic *Queen of the Woods*, America's first Indian novelists were hesitant, unsure of the European vehicle--the novel--then less than two centuries old, and unsure of how to present their subject-matter to a non-Indian audience in a non-Indian language. While Pokagon's novel depicts eloquently if at times awkwardly the difficulty of the Indian in a white-dominated world, a later writer such as Oskison was content in his novels to write adventures set in Indian Territory with very little attention to the Indians--his people--inhabiting that

territory. Although Oskison wrote many short stories
and essays dealing with Indian people, for Oskison,
the Indian is marginal to his portrayal of a developing frontier culture in the Oklahoma Territory. Only
with Mathews' *Sundown* (1934) does the American Indian
protagonist begin to emerge in American Indian fiction
as a complex figure caught between worlds. Writing in
the Hemingway era, Mathews captures in his protagonist
Chal (Challenge) Windzer the naturalistic victim
common to so much twentieth-century fiction, while
simultaneously he introduces the figure which would
come to dominate American Indian fiction: the alienated mixed-blood caught between worlds and identities.
Two years after the publication of *Sundown*, D'Arcy
McNickle provided an even more intense portrayal of
the mixed-blood in *The Surrounded* (1936), a novel
which powerfully depicts the entrapment of the
Flathead (Salish) people in northern Montana and the
inexorable destruction of Archilde Leon, his mixed-
blood protagonist. McNickle, half-blood and Oxford-
educated, stresses the difficulty, verging on impossi-
bility, of communication between Indian and white
worlds, a theme he would pick up once again with even
greater force in his posthumously published *Wind From
An Enemy Sky* (1979).
Although novels about Indians by non-Indian
novelists such as Oliver LaFarge, Hal Borland, and
Frank Waters generated considerable attention in the
middle decades of the century, prior to *House Made of
Dawn's* appearance in 1968 the American Indian novel
had made no significant impact on American literature,
a literature so strongly influenced by regional and
ethnic voices. However, since the publication of
Momaday's novel, works by Indian authors have moved
much closer to the forefront of American fiction,
eclipsing the customary "Indian" novels by white
writers. The voice of these novels is, for the most
part, that of the American writer exploring his or her
position between cultures and turning ever more directly toward the Indian world for a new or renewed
sense of identity and place. Thus Abel, the protagonist of Momaday's sophisticated and modernistic
novel, finds the possibility of renewal and both

physical and psychic survival only in returning to the
Southwest pueblo where he began and immersing himself
once again in the tradition of his people. Thus, the
thrust of Storm's very popular *Seven Arrows* (1972) is
toward a reawakened understanding of the cultural tradition available to contemporary Indians and even non-
Indians as a means of cultural and personal survival,
while in *The Song of Heyoekhah* (1979) Storm merges
vision quest and white initiation into the Indian
world. And thus fourteen-year-old Billy White Hawk in
Janet Campbell Hale's moving novel *The Owl's Song*
(1974) must return to the reservation he has briefly
fled in order to discover a reassuring sense of place
and well-being. In the same vein, Tayo, the half-
breed protagonist of Silko's *Ceremony* (1977), is
healed of the scars of war and displacement only
through immersion in the tradition and ceremonies of
his Indian people, a healing which brings new growth
to both Tayo and the land itself. Similarly, Welch's
unnamed protagonist in the surrealistic, bitter
comedy, *Winter in the Blood* (1974), is allowed a
fleeting glimpse of a world of order and meaning only
in a momentary vision of the way it used to be, of the
world of his grandmother and grandfather, the old
world of the Blackfeet and Gros Ventre. The narrator
of this first Welch novel is alienated from the past,
his Indian heritage, and adrift in a timeless waste-
land world of "stalking white men." In *The Death of
Jim Loney*, Welch's second novel (1979), the half-breed
protagonist is cut off from both past and future,
alienated from both white and Indian worlds, capable
of asserting meaning in his life only by taking up the
position of warrior and forcing the mixed white-and-
Indian society of his small Montana town to destroy
him. James Tucker, in the first two books of his
projected *Stone* trilogy, *Stone: The Birth* (1981) and
Stone: The Journey (1981), takes the reader back to
pre-European times to investigate myth and reality in
the Indian world.

In Gerald Vizenor's *Darkness in Saint Louis
Bearheart* (1978), American Indian fiction has produced
its first post-modern novel, a harsh post-apocalyptic
comedy which breaks with tradition, satirizes itself

and its genre, and nonetheless still asserts the
necessity of rediscovering a nearly lost tradition.
Guided by the spirit of Coyote and Raven, *Darkness in
Saint Louis Bearheart* follows its misfits, clown-
crows, and mixed-blood tricksters across an America
gone berserk toward the center and place of power at
Pueblo Bonito.

In the newest American Indian novel, *The Woman
Who Owned the Shadows* (1983), poet and critic Paula
Gunn Allen gives us the first full-length portrait of
a contemporary Indian woman trapped in the alienated
world of the mixed-blood. In the first published
novel to deal with the contemporary Indian woman from
the Indian woman's point of view, Ephanie, Allen's
protagonist, leads the reader in an agonizing spiritual quest that moves back into the shamanistic world
of her Keres people. Like Momaday and Silko, in particular, Allen weaves the power of traditional mythology and spirituality through her narrative, providing
a dimension unique to American Indian writing. A
similar work may soon appear with the publication of
Janet Campbell Hale's current work-in-progress, a
novel which also follows its female protagonist on a
quest for self-knowledge and survival from the reservation in Idaho to the urban centers of Berkeley and
San Francisco and back again.

Contemporary Indian novelists write with the
sophistication of authors who know both the traditions
of their Indian heritage and the world of twentieth-
century fiction. Stream-of-consciousness, flashback,
surrealism, and absurdism or black humor mingle with
traditional Keres and Blackfeet and Anishinabe
material and allusions to T.S. Eliot, Hemingway,
Beckett, and Faulkner.

Ironically, the birth and development of the
American Indian novel has grown in part from the
enforced process of acculturation, for only through
some degree of assimilation into the non-Indian white
culture have these writers been able to achieve what
they have achieved. To begin with, the Indian novelist has had to adopt not only the English language but
also a relatively new and alien vehicle: the novel
form. And in a survey of the authors included in this

bibliography, it will become readily apparent that
these writers are not ordinary Indians or ordinary
Americans. For the most part, from Simon Pokagon
onward, these men and women are exceptionally well
educated, having studied not only tribal tradition but
also in such universities as Oxford, Harvard,
Stanford, and Berkeley, while earning B.A., M.A., and
Ph.D. degrees. A number, including Bedford, Hale,
McNickle, Momaday, Silko, Vizenor, Welch, and Allen,
have taught or currently teach in American colleges
and universities. Welch has lived and written in
Greece and Mexico, while Vizenor has spent the 1983-84
year teaching at Tiajin University in The People's
Republic of China. Through their growing sophistication and awareness of two worlds, these authors have
been able to bridge the gap between cultures in strik-
ingly successful ways, in both their personal lives
and their fiction. No longer does the Indian of the
American novel merely reflect the common stereotype of
what an Indian is supposed to be; in contemporary
fiction by Indian writers, Indian and non-Indian alike
are permitted to be not stereotypes but individuals
with complex needs, desires, and destinies. Nor does
this new fiction merely protest the lot of the Indian
in America, although it does not ignore the injustice
and callousness of America's treatment of the Indian.
In the works of Momaday, Silko, Welch, Hale, and Allen
in particular, the contemporary Indian protagonist
reflects not only the predicament of the Indian in
modern America, but also the larger predicament of the
sensitive individual in a complex and difficult world,
the predicament of alienated modern man and woman.
And for the first time in the American novel, the
pervasiveness of humor in the Indian world is becoming
apparent in works by such writers as Welch and
Vizenor.

　　Criticism has responded quickly to this renaissance in American Indian fiction. While critics had
largely ignored earlier works of such writers as
Oskison, McNickle, and Mathews, since the appearance
of *House Made of Dawn* a growing critical industry has
sprung up around American Indian writing. As the
citations in this volume will attest, since 1968

scores of articles and reviews dedicated to exploring and analyzing the American Indian novel have appeared in ever-increasing numbers. Critics have been particularly eager to attempt to define the impressive achievements of such writers as Momaday, Welch, and Silko, and a few critics have begun to look more comprehensively at such less-well-known works as those of Pokagon, Hum-Ishu-Ma, McNickle, and Hale.

Even more important as an indication of the emergence of the Indian novel is the fact that since 1978, two booklength studies focused exclusively on Indian novelists have appeared: Charles R. Larson's *American Indian Fiction* (1978) and Alan R. Velie's *Four American Indian Literary Masters* (1982). Larson's book opens the terrain of the Indian novel and lays important groundwork for future studies as it surveys the breadth and scope of Indian novelists from Pokagon to Vizenor. Focusing on Momaday, Welch, Silko, and Vizenor, Velie's study goes into detail not possible in a work of Larson's dimensions. A more comprehensive approach to Indian writing as a whole is Kenneth Lincoln's *Native American Renaissance* (1983), a study which puts the phenomenon of American Indian literature into perspective for us, considering not only the oral tradition from which this literature grows but also the context of twentieth-century American literature in the tradition of the modernists and post modernists. Perhaps the most valuable book to appear for teachers of Indian literature is Paula Gunn Allen's *Studies in American Indian Literature*, which provides insightful introductions and criticism as well as suggested course designs and an excellent bibliography.

L.O.

American Indian Novelists

Paula Gunn Allen
(1939 -)

I. Biography

Born in New Mexico of Laguna, Sioux, and Lebanese-American ancestry, Paula Gunn Allen holds Ph.D., M.F.A. and B.A. degrees. She has served as director of American Indian Studies at San Francisco State University and has taught in the Native American Studies program at the University of California at Berkeley. Paula Gunn Allen's publications include five books of poetry since 1975, critical essays, a volume of essays and course designs, and one novel. In 1978 she received a National Endowment for the Arts grant, and in 1981 a postdoctoral fellowship in American Indian Studies at the University of California, Los Angeles.

II. Primary Sources

Novels

The Woman Who Owned The Shadows. San Francisco: Spinsters, Ink, 1983.
This, Allen's first novel, is also one of the first novels by an Indian writer to explore the world of the mixed-blood Indian woman. In Ephanie Atencio, Allen's protagonist, the author demonstrates the pain of displacement and alienation seemingly inherent in the mixed-blood world as Ephanie travels from New Mexico to San Francisco and the Northwest in search of her own identity and meaning. Gradually, Ephanie rediscovers a structure and meaning in the Keres traditions and mythology of her Pueblo heritage and especially in the creative, regenerative powers of Spider-Woman. In the process, Allen overturns stereotypes--both white and Indian--and develops a modern Indian protagonist of great complexity and sensitivity.

3

Other Booklength Works

The Blind Lion. Berkeley: Thorp Springs, 1975.
Coyote's Daylight Trip. Albuquerque: La
   Confluencia, 1978.
Starchild. Marvin, S.D.: Blue Cloud Quarterly,
   1981.
A Cannon Between My Knees. New York: Straw-
   berry Press, 1981.
Shadow Country. Native American Series. Los
   Angeles: UCLA, 1982.
Studies in American Indian Literature
   (editor). New York: Modern Language
   Association, 1983.

Selected Shorter Publications

Poems

"Catching One Clear Thought Alive." In *The
   Third Woman: Minority Women Writers of the
   United States.* Dexter Fisher, ed. Boxton:
   Houghton Mifflin Co., 1980, 128-129.
"Cowboy." In *A Nation Within: Contemporary
   Native American Writing.* Ralph Salisbury,
   ed. Hamilton, New Zealand: Outrigger
   Publishers, 1983, 48.
"Crow Ambush." In *Four Indian Poets.* John R.
   Milton, ed. University of South Dakota:
   Dakota Press, 1974, 44.
"Deep Deep City Blues: Elegy for the Man Who
   Owned the Rain." In Milton, *Four Indian
   Poets,* 33.
"Dine." In *South Dakota Review,* 12:4, (Winter
   1974-75), 111. Reprint in *I am the Fire of
   Time: The Voices of Native American Women.*
   Jane B. Katz, ed. New York: E.P. Dutton,
   1977, 154-155.
"Grandmother." In *Southwest: A Contemporary
   Anthology.* Karl and Jane Kopp, eds.
   Albuquerque, New Mexico: Red Earth Press,
   1977, 184. Reprint in Fisher, *The Third
   Woman,* 126 and in *Songs From This Earth on*

Turtle's Back. Joseph Bruchac, ed. Greenfield Center, New York: Greenfield Review Press, 1983, 3.

"Hoop Dancer." In Milton, *Four Indian Poets,* 34. Reprint in *The Remembered Earth: An Anthology of Contemporary Native American Literature.* Geary Hobson, ed. Albuquerque, New Mexico: Red Earth Press, 1979, 218.

"Ikce Wichasha." In Milton, *Four Indian Poets,* 35. Reprint in Hobson, *The Remembered Earth,* 218.

"Jet Plane (Dhla-nuwa)." In Milton, *Four Indian Poets,* 47-48.

"Lament of my Father, Lakota." In *South Dakota Review,* 11:1, (Spring 1973), 3. Reprint in *Voices From Wah'Kon-Tah: Contemporary Poetry of Native Americans.* Robert K. Dodge and Joseph B. McCullough, eds. New York: International Publishers, 1974, 25.

"Madonna of the Hills." In Hobson, *The Remembered Earth,* 219.

"Medicine Song." In Milton, *Four Indian Poets,* 36-40. Reprint in Fisher, *The Third Woman,* 129-130.

"Moonshot: 1969." In Fisher, *The Third Woman,* 127-128.

"Mountain Song." In Milton, *Four Indian Poets,* 43.

"Poem for Rat." *Shantih,* 4:1 (Summer-Fall 1979), 17.

"Rain for Ka-waik Bu-ne-ya." In Milton, *Four Indian Poets,* 41-42. Reprint in Hobson, *The Remembered Earth,* 217.

"Riding the Thunder." *Shantih,* 4:2 (Summer-Fall 1979), 16.

"Sandia Crest, May, 1973." In Milton, *Four Indian Poets,* 46.

"The One Who Skins Cats." In *Sinister Wisdom: A Gathering of Spirit.* North American Indian Women's Issue, no. 22-23, Beth Brandt, ed. (1983), 12-17.

"Snowgoose." In Milton, *Four Indian Poets,* 45. Reprint in Hobson, *The Remembered Earth,* 217.

"3/4 Time: Triangulation." In *Salisbury, A
    Nation Within*, 48.
"The Return." *Shantih*, 4:2 (Summer-Fall 1979),
    16.
"Tucson: First Night." In Hobson, *The
    Remembered Earth*, 219.
"Wool Season." In *The American Poetry Review*,
    4:5 (S-O 1975), 46. Reprint in Katz, *I am
    the Fire of Time*, 105-106, and in Kopp and
    Kopp, *Southwest*, 184-185.

Short Fiction

"Ephanie." *Shantih*, 4:2 (Summer-Fall 1979),
    42-47.
"Iyani: It Goes This Way." In Hobson, *The
    Remembered Earth*, 191-193.

Articles and Essays

"A Stranger in My Own Life: Alienation in
    American Indian Prose and Poetry." *MELUS*,
    7:2 (1980), 3-19.
"Answering the Deer: Genocide and Continuance
    in American Indian Women's Poetry."
    *American Indian Culture and Research
    Journal*, 6:1 (1982).
"Beloved Women: Lesbians in American Indian
    Culture." *Conditions*, 7 (Spring 1981), 67-
    87.
"The Feminine Landscape of Leslie Marmon
    Silko's *Ceremony*." *American Indian
    Quarterly*, 5:1 (1979), 7-12.
"The Grace That Remains: American Indian
    Women's Literature." *Book Forum* ("Special
    Issue on American Indians Today"), 5:3
    (1981), 376-83. Reprint as *American Indians
    Today: Thought, Literature, and Art*. New
    York: Horizon, 1982.
"The Sacred Hoop: A Contemporary Indian
    Perspective on American Literature." In
    *Literature of the American Indians: Views
    and Interpretations*. Abraham Chapman, ed.

New York: New American Library, 1975, 111-
135. Reprint in *The Remembered Earth: An
Anthology of Contemporary Native American
Literature.* Geary Hobson, ed. Albuquerque,
New Mexico: Red Earth Press, 1979, 222-239.

III. Selected Secondary Sources

Criticism

Ruoff, A. LaVonne Brown. *Studies in American
Indian Literatures: Newsletter of the
Association For Study of American Indian
Literatures,* 8:3 (Fall 1983), 65-69.
In this critical review based on a manuscript
version of *The Woman Who Owned The Shadows,*
Ruoff describes the novel as "the journey toward spiritual rebirth," and declares that
"the novel describes Ephanie's quest for spiritual powers." While stressing the "skillful
portraits of feminine relationships" in the
novel, Ruoff simultaneously details the
author's interweaving of Keres mythology "to
demonstrate the parallelism between the mythic
experiences of Keres deities and those of
Ephanie." Ruoff finds parallels between Ephanie and Spider Woman's descendents, especially
Iyatiku, Corn Woman, and Kochinninaku, Yellow
woman. Ruoff also briefly notes the theme of
alienation brought about by Ephanie's mixed-
blood heritage and isolation between cultures,
and comments upon the novel's autobiographical
quality.

Biographical Sources

*An Annotated Bibliography: Literature by and
About the American Indian,* ed. by Anna Lee
Stensland. Urbana, Illinois: National
Council of Teachers of English, 1979.

Songs From This Earth on Turtle's Back:
  Contemporary American Indian Poetry, ed. by
  Joseph Bruchac. Greenfield Center, New
  York: The Greenfield Review Press, 1983.
Voices From Wah' Kon-tah, ed. by Robert K.
  Dodge and Joseph B. McCulloch. New York:
  International Publishers, 1974.

Denton R. Bedford
(1907-)

I. Biography

In his own words "somewhat more than one-quarter Minsi (Munsee) Indian," Denton R. Bedford is descended through his father, Sitamaganend, of Chief Wapalanewa, a famous pro-British raider during the American Revolution. Bedford, whose Minsi name is Wapalanewa, earned B.S. and M.S. degrees in history from Lafayette College and continued his graduate study at Columbia University. For more than twenty years, Bedford taught both high school and college history.

II. Primary Sources

Novels

Tsali. San Francisco: The Indian Historian Press, 1972.
Bedford's historical novel centers around Tsali, a Cherokee who kills one of his guards and escapes with his family as the Cherokee people are being rounded up for the Removal to the Indian Territories in the West. In the mountain wilderness where they are hiding, Tsali and his family meet other Cherokees who have escaped from the stockades and who are desperately trying to survive and avoid the government patrols searching for them. In the end, Tsali and his sons and brother surrender to the government forces to avoid the slaughter of the remaining free Cherokee and are quickly executed. Bedford adds frequent historical information and authorial commentary to his fictionalized account of this authentic Cherokee hero.

III. Selected Secondary Sources

Criticism

Larson, Charles R. *American Indian Fiction.*
Albuquerque, University of New Mexico
Press, 1978, 126-132.
Larson provides a brief discussion of *Tsali*,
finding that the "emotional core of the narrative" is Tsali's private war with the U.S. government and that the many authorial intrusions
"destroy the dramatic tension of the novel."
Larson further argues that Bedford's didactic
tone "denies the novel much subtlety," and that
the white characters are stereotyped. Larson
compares Tsali to the protagonists of *Winter
Count* and *Seven Arrows*, suggesting that these
Indian protagonists "retain a basic affinity with
their people," and that "they fulfill the heroic
call by moving to assume the vital center of the
spiritual whole."

Rosen, Kenneth. "American Indian Literature:
Current Condition and Suggested Research."
*American Indian Culture and Research
Journal*, 3 (1979), 57-66.
In this survey essay, Rosen calls *Tsali* "a
carefully focused novel" and states that Tsali's
"heroic nature and . . . complex relationship to
his people . . . is consistently interesting and
well handled . . . ." Rosen suggests, however,
that Bedford overloads the narrative with
historical data to the detriment of the novel.

Dallas Chief Eagle
(1925 - 1978)

I. Biography

Dallas Chief Eagle was born on the Rosebud Reservation in South Dakota. Orphaned as a child, he was brought up by the elders of the tribe. He was chosen by the Teton Sioux as chief in 1967, the first Teton Sioux chief since Red Cloud was chosen in 1868. He was also the director of tourism of the Development Corporation of the United Sioux Tribes of South Dakota. Chief Eagle has published one novel, *Winter Count*, and has assisted in a biography, *Fools Crow*.

II. Primary Sources

Novels

> *Winter Count.* Colorado Springs, Colorado: Dentan-Berkeland Printing, Co., Inc., 1967. Reprint Denver: Golden Bell Press, 1968; reprint Boulder, Colorado: Johnson Publishing Co., 1968.

The framing device of this panoramic novel is the search of Turtleheart for his wive Evensigh, who has been stolen by runaway white soldiers shortly after the young Sioux's marriage. Evensigh, who is white but has grown up with the Teton Sioux, is taken to the East and adopted by a white family. Chief Eagle manages to telescope a large portion of the events and history of the Indian wars of the second half of the nineteenth century into the novel, including the Battle of the Little Bighorn and the reduction of the Cheyenne and Sioux to the status of impoverished government retainers.

Other Booklength Works

Fools Crow. Recorded by Thomas E. Mails,
assisted by Dallas Chief Eagle. Garden
City, New York: Doubleday and Co., 1979.

Selected Shorter Publications

Short Fiction

"Blood on the Little Bighorn" (excerpt from
Winter Count). In *American Indian Authors*.
Natachee Scott Momaday, ed. Boston:
Houghton Mifflin Co., 1972, 30-37.

III. Selected Secondary Sources

Criticism of *Winter Count*

Larson, Charles R. *American Indian Fiction*.
Albuquerque: University of New Mexico
Press, 100-112.
Larson defines Turtleheart's role in the novel as
that of "the observer of the times during which
he lives . . . ." Larson calls Chief Eagle a
"syncretist," suggesting that the author believes
in blending Indian and non-Indian cultures. This
critic sees the dying Turtleheart's acquiescence
to Christianity as pessimistic, declaring that
"the whites have won both the literal and the
symbolic war with the Indians," and he defines
the pessimism of the novel as "a pessimism
inherent in the reality of the historical events
. . . ."

Biographical Sources

Steiger, Brad. "Dallas Chief Eagle - Spiritual
Warrier of the Sioux." In Steiger, *Medicine
Talk: A Guide to Walking in Balance and
Surviving on the Earth Mother*. New York:
Doubleday and Co., Inc., 1975, 106-132.

Janet Campbell Hale
(1946-)

I. Biography

Janet Campbell Hale is a member of the Coeur d'Alene tribe of northern Idaho and is also part Kootenai on her mother's side. Born in Riverside, California, Hale attended the Institute of American Indian Arts in Santa Fe from 1962-1964 and graduated from the University of California at Berkeley in 1974. She has taught at U.C. Berkeley, U.C. Davis, and D.Q. University in Davis, California, and studied law at both U.C. Berkeley and Gonzaga Law School in Spokane, Washington. Hale currently teaches at Lummi Community College in the state of Washington while completing a second novel.

II. Primary Sources

Novels

The Owl's Song. Garden City: Doubleday, 1974. Reprint Avon, 1975.
Fourteen-year-old Billy White Hawk grows up on the reservation in Idaho living in poverty with his alcoholic father. After Billy graduates from the local school, he leaves the reservation to live in a big city with his older half-sister and attend high school. Billy faces daily hostility and persecution in the urban school until he finally decides to return to his father and the reservation. The novel ends with Billy discovering a secure sense of belonging once he has returned to his home and people.

Other Booklength Works

Custer Lives in Humboldt County. Greenfield Center, New York: Greenfield Review Press, 1976.

Selected Shorter Publications

Poems

"Aaron Nicholas, Almost Ten." In *Voices of the
Rainbow: Contemporary Poetry by American
Indians.* Kenneth Rosen, ed. New York,
Seaver Books, 1975, 52. Reprint in Hale,
Custer Lives in Humboldt County. Greenfield
Center, New York: Greenfield Review Press,
1978, 5, and in *The Third Woman: Minority
Women Writers of the United States.* Dexter
Fisher, ed. Boston: Houghton Mifflin Co.,
1980, 108.

"Alligator Bites." In Hale, *Custer Lives in
Humboldt County,* 6, and in *The Next World:
Poems by 33 Third World Americans.* Joseph
Bruchac, ed. Trumansburg, New York: The
Crossing Press, 1978, 63.

"At an Aztec Pyramid Just Outside Mexico
City." In Hale, *Custer Lives in Humboldt
County,* 22.

"Beverly." In *Custer Lives in Humboldt County,*
11.

"Cinque." In Rosen, *Voices of the Rainbow,* 51.

"Custer Lives in Humboldt County." In Rosen,
Voices of the Rainbow, 54. Reprint in
Bruchac, *Songs From This Earth on Turtle's
Back,* 89, and in Hale, *Custer Lives in
Humboldt County,* 1.

"Desmet, Idaho, March, 1969." In Rosen, *Voices
of the Rainbow,* 49. Reprint in Hale, *Custer
Lives in Humboldt County,* 21; in Fisher,
The Third Woman, 107; and Bruchac, *Songs
From This Earth On Turtle's Back,* 88.

"Getting Started." In Rosen, *Voices of the
Rainbow,* 50.

"My Sisters The Summer of '53." In Hale,
Custer Lives in Humboldt County, 4, and in
Bruchac, *The Next World,* 63-64.

"Nespelim Man." In *The Whispering Wind: Poetry
by Young American Indians.* Terry Allen, ed.
New York: Doubleday, 1972, 32. Reprint in

Voices from Wah'Kon-Tah: Contemporary Poetry of Native Americans. Robert K. Dodge and Joseph B. McCullough, eds. New York: International Publishers, 1974, 36.

"Nursing Home Patient." In Hale, *Custer Lives in Humboldt County*, 18.

"On a Catholic Childhood." In Rosen, *Voices of the Rainbow*, 47. Reprint in Hale, *Custer Lives in Humboldt County*, 9, and in Fisher, *The Third Woman*, 106-107.

"On Death and Love." In Rosen, *Voices of the Rainbow*, 53. Reprint in Hale, *Custer Lives in Humboldt County*, 19.

"Our Friend, the Virgin Mary." In *The Remembered Earth: An Anthology of Native American Literature.* Geary Hobson, ed. Albuquerque, N.M.: Red Earth Press, 1979, 410.

"Red Eagle." In Allen, *The Whispering Wind*, 32. Reprint in Dodge and McCullough, *Voices From Wah'Kon-Tah*, 35.

"Salad La Raza." In Rosen, *Voices of the Rainbow*, 46. Reprint in Hale, *Custer Lives in Humboldt County.*

"Scene From A Dream." In Bruchac, *Songs From This Earth On Turtle's Back*, 87.

"Six Feet Under." In Rosen, *Voices of the Rainbow*, 52. Reprint in Hale, *Custer Lives in Humboldt County*, 3.

"Sleeping Children." In Hale, *Custer Lives in Humboldt County*, 24.

"The Snow Keeps Falling." In Fisher, *The Third Woman*, 54-57.

"To A Recently Retired Supreme Court Justice." In Hale, *Custer Lives in Humboldt County*, 13-17.

"Tribal Cemetery." In Hale, *Custer Lives in Humboldt County*, 7, and in Bruchac, *The Next World*, 64-65.

"Walls of Ice." In Bruchac, *Songs From This Earth On Turtle's Back*, 86.

"Where Have All The Indians Gone." In Bruchac, *Songs From This Earth On Turtle's Back*, 90.

Short Fiction

"From *The Only Good Indian*" (excerpt from
novel-in-progress). In Hobson, *The
Remembered Earth*, 408-410.

III. **Selected Secondary Sources**

Criticism of *The Owl's Song*

Rosen, Kenneth. "American Indian
Literature: Current Condition and
Suggested Research." *American Indian
Culture and Research Journal*, 3 (1979), 57-
66.
In this review article, Rosen touches briefly
upon *The Owl's Song*, calling the novel "a
touching and often powerful story of a young
boy's attempt to survive in a world that seems
determined to destroy him . . . ."

Reviews of *The Owl's Song*

Akwesasne Notes. Volume 7, Early Winter 1975,
45.
Booklist. Volume 70, July 1, 1974, 1194.
Best Sellers. Volume 34, May 15, 1974, 101.
Center for Children's Books Bulletin. Volume
27, July 1974, 178.
Kirkus Reviews. Volume 42, April 1, 1974, 372.
Library Journal. Volume 99, September 15,
1974, 2290.
New York Times Book Review. August 25, 1974, 8

Biographical Sources

*Contemporary Authors: A Bio-Bibliographical
Guide to Current Authors and Their Works,*
ed. by Clare D. Kinsman. Detroit: Gale
Research Co., 1975.

Literature By and About the American Indian:
An Annotated Bibliography, ed. by Anna Lee
Stensland. Urbana, Illinois: National
Council of Teachers of English, 1979.
The Next World: Poems by 32 Third World
Americans, ed. by Joseph Bruchac.
Trumansburg, New York: The Crossing Press,
1978.
Songs From This Earth On Turtle's Back:
Contemporary American Indian Poetry, ed. by
Joseph Bruchac. Greenfield Center, New
York: The Greenfield Review Press, 1983.
Voices From Wah'Kon-tah, ed. by Robert K.
Dodge and Joseph B. McCullough. New York:
International Publishers, 1974.
The Whispering Wind, ed. by Terry D. Allen.
Garden City, New York: Doubleday, 1972.

Jamake Highwater
(1942 -)

I. **Biography**

Jamake Highwater, who describes himself as part Blackfeet and Cherokee, was born in Glacier County, Montana. One of the most widely published of American Indian writers, Highwater has written on subjects as diverse as Indian affairs, Indian culture and art, travel, and popular culture. Highwater has served as Consultant on American Indians to the New York Council on the Arts and is a member of the White Buffalo Council of American Indians. He has published two booklength works of fiction in addition to numerous non-fiction works as Jamake Highwater and J. Marks and has won numerous awards for his writing. *Anpao: An American Indian Odyssey* has been named a Newberry Honor Book, while *Many Smokes, Many Moons* received the Jane Addams Book Award in 1979, awarded by the Women's International League for Peace and Freedom.

II. **Primary Sources**

Novels

> *Anpao: An American Indian Odyssey.* New
> York: Lippincott, 1977.
> Anpao is in love with Ko-ko-mik-e-is, but she is already promised to the Sun. Anpao's adventures as he journeys to the Sun to obtain permission to marry Ko-ko-mik-e-is weave Highwater's fiction with legends of the northern plains and southwestern U.S.

> *The Sun He Dies.* New York: Lippincott and
> Crowell, 1980.
> Highwater's second novel, this work of historical fiction is set in Tenochtitlan, the Aztec capital

at the time of the Spanish invasion of the Aztec
empire. Although told through the character of
Nanautzin, a woodcutter and spokesman for
Montezuma II, the novel deals primarily with
Montezuma's belief in the return of Quetzalcoatl
and the effects this belief has on Montezuma's
reaction to the invading Cortez.

Other Booklength Works

(Under pseudonym, J. Marks) *Rock and Other
Four Letter Words.* New York: Bantam, 1969.
(Under pseudonym, J. Marks) *Mick Jagger: The
Singer Not the Song.* Indianapolis: Curtis
Books, 1973.
Indian America: A Cultural Guide. New York:
McKay, 1975.
*Song From the Earth: American Indian
Painting.* Boston: Little, Brown, 1976.
*Ritual of the Wind: North American Indian
Ceremonies, Music, and Dances.* New York:
Viking Press, 1977.
Dance: Rituals of Experience. New York: A &
W Publishers, 1978.
Journey to the Sky. New York: T.Y. Crowell,
1978.
*Many Smokes, Many Moons: A Chronology of
American Indian History through Indian Art.*
New York: Lippincott, 1978.
*The Sweet Grass Lives On: Fifty Contemporary
American Indian Artists.* New York:
Lippincott and Crowell, 1980.
Moon Song Lullaby. New York: Lothrop, Lee and
Shepard Books, 1981.
*The Primal Mind: Vision and Reality in Indian
America.* New York: Harper and Row, 1981.

Selected Shorter Publications

Articles and Essays

"The Sweet Grass Lives On." *Shantih,* 4:2
(Summer-Fall 1979), 14-15.

III. Selected Secondary Sources

Criticism of *Anpao*

Hunter, Carol. "American Indian Literature."
MELUS, 8:2 (Summer 1981), 82-85.
Hunter asserts that "American Indian writers in
the 1980's project tribal ethos, regional
identity, and their cultural heritage" from
traditional oral literature. She divides
American Indian literature into the categories of
traditional oral literature and modern fiction,
and in a brief treatment of *Anpao* she points out
that Highwater begins the story with an origin
tale, "Split Boy," and that he incorporates "a
variety of Native American folktales while
focusing on the main character of Anpao."

Reviews

Anpao
    Booklist. Volume 74, November 15, 1977, 542.
    Book World. February 12, 1978, G4.
    Book World. December 10, 1978, E5.
    Center for Children's Books Bulletin. Volume
       31, March 1978,
    Childhood Education. Volume 55, October 1978,
       38.
    Catholic Library World. Volume 49, December
       1977, 325.
    Catholic Library World. Volume 50, October
       1978, 109.
    Horn Book Magazine. Volume 54, February 1978,
       55.
    Journal of Reading. Volume 22, November 1978,
       184.
    Kirkus Reviews. Volume 45, October 1, 1977,
       1053.
    Language Arts. Volume 55, February 1978, 213.
    New York Times Book Review, February 5, 1978,
       26.
    School Library Journal. Volume 24, October
       1977, 124.

School Library Journal. Volume 26, November
1979, 43.
Teacher. Volume 95, May 1978, 100

The Sun He Dies
American Indian Quarterly. Volume 5, November
1979, 367-68.

Biographical Sources

Aston, John. "Tempest in a Tepee." *Westward,*
17:12 (1983).
*Contemporary Authors: A Bio-Bibliographical
Guide to Current Authors and Their Works,*
vol. 65-68, ed. by Clare D. Kinsman.
Detroit: Gale Research Co., 1977.
Contemporary Literary Criticism, vol. 12.
Detroit: Gale Research Co., 1980.
*Literature By and About the American Indian:
An Annotated Bibliography,* ed. by Anna Lee
Stensland. Urbana, Illinois: National
Council of Teachers of English, 1979.
National Playwrights Directory, The O'Neill
Theater Center, 1977.
Who's Who in America, 42nd edition, vol. 2
(1982-83). Chicago: Marquis Who's Who, Inc.

Hum-Ishu-Ma
(Mourning Dove; Cristal McLeod Galler)
(1888 - 1936)

I. Biography

Mourning Dove, an Okanogan Indian, was born near Bonner's Ferry, Idaho, to Joseph Quintasket and Lucy Stukin. Mourning Dove attended Sacred Heart Convent in Ward, Washington very briefly as a child and later studied at government schools and a business school. Her formal education was minimal. Married twice, Mourning Dove worked as a migrant farm laborer while writing her novel and collection of coyote stories. She was an honorary member of the Eastern Washington State Historical Society and a life member of the Washington State Historical Society.

II. Primary Sources

Novels

> *Co-Ge-We-A, The Half-Blood: A Depiction of the Great Montana Cattle Range, by Hum-ishu-ma, "Mourning Dove," . . .Given through Sho-pow-tan.* With Notes and Biographical Sketch by Lucullus Virgil McWhorter. Boston: Four Seas Co., 1927. Reprint with introduction by Dexter Fisher, Lincoln: University of Nebraska Press, 1981.

The protagonist of this, Mourning Dove's only novel, is Cogewea, whose mother is Okanogan and whose father is a white man named Bertram McDonnald. The setting is the Horseshoe Bend Ranch on the Pend d'Oreille River. Jim LaGrinder, a half-blood and the ranch foreman, is in love with Cogewea, who has "eyes of the deepest jet" and hair "as lustrous as the raven's wing." Cogewea, however, falls for the

attractions of a non-Indian scoundrel named
Alfred Densmore, and most of the novel's plot
consists of Cogewea discovering that Densmore is
a culprit and LaGrinder the right man for her.
The conflict between Indian and white is also a
central theme in the book, with the character
with both Indian and white ancestry described as
"a breed! The socially ostracized of two races."

Other Booklength Works

> *Coyote Stories.* With Notes by Lucullus Virgil
>   McWhorter. Foreword by Chief Standing Bear.
>   Ed. Heister Dean Gurie. Caldwell, Idaho:
>   The Caston Printers, 1933. Reprint New
>   York: AMS, 1977.
> *The Tales of the Okanogans.* Ed. Donald M.
>   Hines. Fairfield, Washington: Ye Galleon,
>   1976.

III. Selected Secondary Sources

Criticism of *Cogewea*

> Fisher, Dexter. Introduction to *Cogewea, The
>   Half-Blood: A Depiction of the Great
>   Montana Cattle Range.* Lincoln: University
>   of Nebraska Press, 1981, v-xxix.

In this introduction to the 1981 reprint of
Cogewea, Fisher documents and analyzes what she
terms the "fascinating collaboration" between
Mourning Dove and Lucullus V. McWhorter, the
Show-pow-tan of the novel's title page. Although
describing McWhorter as a man "of the utmost
integrity," Fisher suggests that it is McWhorter
who is responsible for the novel's intrusive
didacticism and often irrelevant historical
information. The result, according to Fisher, is
that "the narrative, which is very much within
the tradition of the western romance, with its
stock characters and melodrama, sags at times
under the weight of vituperation." Fisher also

points to McWhorter's inclusion in the novel of
his own research as well as his responsibility
for much of the novel's inflated language. In
spite of all this, Fisher concludes that "perhaps
the most that can be said is that neither
Mourning Dove nor McWhorter could have written
the book without the other." In addition to a
thorough discussion of the collaboration, Fisher
provides biographical information about Mourning
Dove and a discussion of Okanogon culture,
especially as it is reflected in the novel.

Larson, Charles, R. *American Indian Fiction*.
Albuquerque: University of New Mexico
Press, 1978, 5, 173-180.
Larson deals with *Cogewea* in an appendix to his
booklength study of Indian novelists "because the
title page identifies a collaborator," a fact
which, states Larson, suggests "a collaboration
or filtering of the original text through another
consciousness." Larson finds the theme of
assimilation central to *Cogewea* and declares that
the "racial theme" is ubiquitous in the story.
Labeling the novel "sentimental and stylized"
Larson further declares that the author(s)
obfuscates the ending by "preaching one thing
while having her characters do another." Larson
finds fault with the novel's "strange blend of
the comic and the serious," and implies that this
may be the result of the collaboration suggested
on the novel's title page.

Biographical Sources

Fisher, Dexter. Introduction to *Cogewea, The
Half-Blood: A Depiction of the Great
Montana Cattle Range*. Lincoln: University
of Nebraska Press, 1981, v-xxix.
Fisher, Dexter. "The Transformation of
Tradition: A Study of Zikala-Sa and
Mourning Dove, Two Transitional Indian
Writers." Dissertation, City University of
New York, 1979.

D'Arcy McNickle
(1904 - 77)

I. Biography

A Creek by blood, McNickle was born in St.
Ignatius, Montana, on the Flathead Reservation,
and adopted into the Confederated Salish and
Kootenai Tribes. He attended mission schools
before going on to public schools and eventually
the University of Montana, Oxford University, and
the University of Grenoble. In addition to
publishing three novels (one posthumously) and a
number of nonfiction works dealing with American
Indians, McNickle was very active in Indian
affairs, co-founding the National Congress of
American Indians and serving from 1936 to 1952 as
director of the Branch of Tribal Relations of the
Bureau of Indian Affairs. He also taught as
professor of anthropology at the University of
Saskatchewan and served as program director of
the Center for American Indian History at the
Newberry Library in Chicago.

II. Primary Sources

Novels

    The Surrounded. New York: Dodd, Mead and
        Co., 1936. Reprint: Macmillan, 1951;
        University of New Mexico Press, 1978.
Archilde Leon, son of a Salish (Flathead) mother
and Spanish father, returns to his father's ranch
after having supported himself for a year in
Oregon as a fiddle player. The division in the
novel between the worlds of Indian and white is
symbolized in the division within Archilde's own
family: while his father, Max Leon, lives in the
big ranch house, his mother lives in a small log
cabin nearby. Gradually, Archilde is trapped in
the destructive confrontation between the Indian
and white worlds as his wild brother is killed by

25

a game warden and his mother in turn kills the
warden. Finally, Archilde is implicated in the
murder of the sheriff who is investigating the
earlier murders, and the novel ends with Archilde
shackled for the crime.

Runner in the Sun: A Story of Indian Maize.
New York: Holt, 1954.
The hero of this novel is a young Indian boy,
Salt, who lives in the canyon country of the
Southwest centuries before Columbus. Because of
an intrigue between clans in the pueblo, Salt
must journey to the land of the Aztecs to procure
a hardier strain of maize. Salt has adventures
enroute and returns with both the corn and a
young slave girl as his wife. This novel is
generally considered as appropriate for juvenile
readers.

Wind From An Enemy Sky. New York: Harper and
Row, 1979.
In this posthumously published novel, McNickle
tells the story of Antoine and his grandfather,
Bull, chief of their small Northwestern tribe,
and of Bull's inexorable entrapment within the
destructive conflict between the old world of the
tribe and the modern world of the white man.
Bull has bitterly opposed the dam which the
government has constructed in the sacred
mountains, and he opposes assimilation into the
white culture surrounding the tribe. The
situation darkens when a member of the tribe
murders the nephew of the dam's well-intentioned
but naive builder, and when Bull and others from
the tribe come to the Indian agency to reclaim
the lost Feather Boy, the tribe's most powerful
medicine bundle, the situation quickly
degenerates into misunderstanding and violent
death in the novel's final scene.

Other Booklength Works

*The Indian Tribes of the United States: Ethnic
and Cultural Survival.* New York: Oxford
University Press, 1962.
*Indians and Other Americans: Two Ways of Life
Meet.* New York: Harper and Row, 1970.
Indian Man: A Life of Oliver LaFarge.
Bloomington: Indiana University Press,
1971.
*They Came Here First: The Epic of the
American Indian.* Philadelpha: J.B.
Lippincott Co., 1949. Reprint Octagon,
1972.
*Native American Tribalism: Indian Survival
and Renewals.* New York: Oxford University
Press, 1973.

III. Selected Secondary Sources

Criticism

The Surrounded
Larson, Charles, R. *American Indian Fiction.*
Albuquerque: University of New Mexico
Press, 1978, p. 68-78.
Larson labels *The Surrounded* "the work of a
gifted writer," and declares that "McNickle is
the earliest Native American prose stylist, the
earliest craftsman of the novel form." Larson
praises McNickle's skillful incorporation of
traditional materials into the narrative and his
sophisticated handling of form, which, according
to Larson, places McNickle stylistically and
thematically in the ranks of American Indian
writers of the 1960's and 1970's rather than with
writers of his own chronological time.

Oaks, Priscilla. "The First Generation of
Native American Novelists." *MELUS*, 5:1
(Spring 1978), p. 57-65.

In an essay discussing the effects of assimilationist policies and a new reader interest in
Indian literature of the thirties, Oaks states
that McNickle was the "most important Native
American writer" of that decade. She suggests
that *The Surrounded* demonstrates the tragedy that
occurs in both Indian and white cultures "when
they become isolated from one another."
According to Oaks, Archilde "shoulders the
symbolic burden of past Indian-American hatred
and acts out again the destruction of the Indian
by the white man." Oaks concludes that "As an
Indian novelist, McNickle saw nothing romantic
about Indian life in America, nor about American
life in general."

Owens, Louis D. "The 'Map of the Mind':
    D'Arcy McNickle and the American Indian
    Novel." *Western American Literature*, 19:3
    (November 1984).
In this discussion of both *The Surrounded* and
Wind From an Enemy Sky, Owens declares that in
these two novels, published more than four
decades apart "McNickle has given us remarkable
perspectives on two 'maps of the mind'--Indian
and white--and his conclusion in both novels is
that the maps simply do not match ...." Owens
focuses on the theme of miscommunication and
misunderstanding in both novels, concluding that
"For McNickle's displaced Indians understanding
fails, speech breaks down, and the result is
alienation and tragedy which the best of inten-
tions--Indian or white--cannot forestall."

Stensland, Anna Lee. "Indian Literature and
    the Adolescent." *Identity and Awareness in
    the Minority Experience*: Selected
    Proceedings of the 1st and 2nd Annual
    Conferences on Minority Studies. La
    Crosse: Institute for Minority Studies,
    University of Wisconsin, 1975, p. 138-54.
In an essay which discusses the dearth of serious
study of Indian literature in primary and

secondary schools, Stensland provides possible
outlines for the study of Indian literature in
both junior and senior high schools. Stensland
recommends *Runner in the Sun* as a novel for
adolescents, giving a plot summary of the novel
and stating, "The book has action and intrigue
and at the same time informs the student about
recognized theories of ancient Indian life."

Wind From An Enemy Sky

Ortiz, Simon J. "Towards a National Indian
Literature: Cultural Authenticity in
Nationalism." *MELUS*, 8:2 (Summer 1981), p.
7-12.
Ortiz's general thesis in this essay is that by
incorporating non-Indian religions and languages
into their own cultures, American Indians "have
creatively responded to forced colonization." He
defines this creative response as one of
resistance. Ortiz defines *Wind From An Enemy Sky*
as "not only a panorama of the early 20th century
as experienced by the Little Elk people but also
of the national Indian experience." Ortiz points
out that McNickle allows the reader to see both
through Antoine's "immediate youthful eyes" and
through the knowledge related by the boy's
grandfather and other kinfolk as well.

Rosen, Kenneth. "American Indian
Literature: Current Condition and
Suggested Research." *American Indian
Culture and Research Journal*, 3:2 (1979),
p. 57-66.
In this survey of American Indian literature,
Rosen briefly notes *Wind From An Enemy Sky* and
states that "it is certainly a work that deserves
careful scholarly attention." Rosen suggests
that the novel be considered in the context of
McNickle's two earlier novels.

Reviews

The Surrounded
   Booklist. Volume 32, April 1936, p. 233.
   Books. February 23, 1936, p. 2.
   Boston Transcript. March 4, 1936, p. 3.
   Current History. Volume 14, April 1936, p. 44.
   New Republic. Volume 86, April 15, 1936, p.
      295.
   New York Herald Tribune. February 14, 1936, p.
      15.
   New York Times. February 16, 1936, p. 7.
   Review of Reviews. Volume 93, April 1936, p.
      21.
   Reprint Bulletin Book Reviews. Volume 23, No.
      3, 1978, p. 33.

Runner in the Sun
   Chicago Sunday Tribune. November 14, 1954, p.
      38.
   Christian Science Monitor. November 11, 1954,
      p. 16.
   Kirkus Reviews. Volume 22, August 15, 1954, p.
      538.
   Library Journal. Volume 79, December 15, 1954,
      p. 2501.
   New York Herald Tribune Book Review. Pt. 2,
      November 14, 1954, p. 26.
   Saturday Review. Volume 37, November 13, 1954,
      p. 90.

Wind From An Enemy Sky
   World Literature Today. Volume 53, Spring,
      1979, p. 247.
   Kirkus Reviews. Volume 46, September 1, 1978,
      p. 967.
   Kirkus Reviews. Volume 46, September 15, 1978,
      p. 1023.
   Library Journal. Volume 103, November 1, 1978,
      p. 2262.
   Publishers Weekly. Volume 214, August 28,
      1978, p. 388.

Markoosie
(1942 -)

I. Biography

Markoosie's full name is Markoosie Patsang. An Inuit Eskimo, Markoosie lives deep inside the Arctic Circle at Resolute Bay and is an arctic pilot--the first Canadian Eskimo to hold a commercial flying license--who flies charter trips and has been active in public services in Canada. Markoosie's single novel, *Harpoon of the Hunter*, first appeared in the newsletter *Inuttituut*, published by the Cultural Development Division of the Department of Indian Affairs and Northern Development in Canada. The novel was first written and published in syllabics and later translated by Markoosie for publication in English. It is the first long work of Eskimo fiction to be published in English.

II. Primary Sources

Novels

> *Harpoon of the Hunter*. Montreal: McGill-
> Queen's University Press, 1970.

The novel tells the story of 16-year-old Kamik, who goes with his father and all but two of the hunters in their small camp to hunt for a rabid and dangerous polar bear which has attacked the camp. In the course of the hunt, Kamik's father and all of the other hunters are killed, leaving only Kamik to struggle across the ice toward home. After a terrible ordeal, Kamik is rescued by neighboring villagers. He falls in love (at first sight) with Putooktee, a girl from the neighboring village, but while crossing the dangerous channel between the villages, Putooktee, along with her father and Kamik's mother, falls through the ice and dies. Kamik, in despair, allows himself to drift away on an ice floe, and

the novel ends with the grim scene of Kamik cut-
ting his throat with his harpoon.

III. **Selected Secondary Sources**

Reviews of *Harpoon of the Hunter*

AB Bookman's Weekly. Volume 47, January 25,
1971.
Atlantic Monthly. Volume 227, January 1971, p.
104.
Center for Children's Books Bulletin. Volume
24, May 1971, p. 141.
Canadian Forum. Volume 51, June 1971, p. 33.
Canadian Geographical Journal. Volume 83,
August 1971, p. R4.
Publishers Weekly. Volume 198, September 28,
1970, p. 72.
Publishers Weekly. Volume 199, January 11,
1971, p. 63.
Times Literary Supplement. March 12, 1971, p.
285.

John Joseph Mathews
(1895 -)

I. **Biography**

John Joseph Mathews, a member of the Osage tribe,
was born in Pawhuska, Oklahoma, in what was then
the center of the Osage Nation. Mathews studied
geology at the University of Oklahoma and graduated in 1920 after a hiatus due to World War I
service as an aviator in France. After gradua-
tion from the University of Oklahoma, Mathews
enrolled at Oxford to study natural science and
received a B.A. from that University in 1923.
Made financially independent by Osage oil rights,
Mathews continued his education at the School of
International Relations at the University of
Geneva, where he received a certificate in 1924.
Mathews traveled widely before returning to Oklahoma to begin his career as writer and recorder
of Osage culture. His first book, *Wah'Kon-Tah*,
was the first work by a university press to be
chosen as a selection by the Book-of-the-Month
Club. Though only one-eighth Osage, Mathews
received 560 acres and a headright when Osage
land was allotted in 1906, and he later served on
the Osage Tribal Council.

II. **Primary Sources**

Novels

> *Sundown.* New York: Longmans, Green and Co.,
> 1934. Reprint Boston: Gregg Press, 1979.
Chal (Challenge) Windzer, son of a mixed-blood
father and full-blood Osage mother, grows up
confused between the Indian and white worlds.
Oil money has brought wealth to the Osage and
destruction to the old ways, and when Chal's
father commits suicide Chal inherits $25,000
which has come from the sale of oil on tribal
land. Chal attends college and enlists in the

air force, but in the end he returns to the
reservation, still trapped ambiguously between
Indian and white worlds.

Other Booklength Works

*Wah'Kon-Tah: The Osage and the White Man's
Road.* Norman: University of Oklahoma
Press, 1932. Reprint 1968.
Talking to the Moon. Chicago: University of
Chicago Press, 1945. Reprint Norman:
University of Oklahoma Press, 1981.
*Life and Death of an Oilman: The Career of
E.W. Marland.* Norman: University of
Oklahoma Press, 1952.
The Osages: Children of the Middle Waters.
Norman: University of Oklahoma Press,
1961.

Selected Shorter Publications

Articles and Essays

"We Are Fed Like Dogs" (excerpt from *Wah'Kon-
Tah*). In *Forgotten Pages of American
Literature.* Gerald Haslam, ed. Boston:
Houghton Mifflin Co., 1970, 38-46.

Interviews

"John Joseph Mathews - A Conversation." Guy
Logsdon. *Nimrod*, 16 (1972), 70-75.

III. Selected Secondary Sources

Criticism of *Sundown*

Hunter, Carol. "American Indian Literature."
MELUS, 8:2, (Summer 1981), 82-85.
Hunter divides American Indian literature into
the categories of traditional oral literature and
modern fiction and asserts that "American Indian

writers in the 1980's project tribal ethos,
regional identity, and their cultural heritage"
from the traditional oral literature. Hunter
mentions Mathews briefly, pointing out that like
other Indian writers such as McNickle, Simon
Ortiz, and Wendy Rose, Mathews reflects a
"regional ethos" in his fiction.

Larson, Charles R. *American Indian Fiction*.
    Albuquerque: University of New Mexico
    Press, 1978.
Larson provides a thorough summary of *Sundown* and
observes that there is little plot to the novel,
that plot has "given way to character development." According to Larson's reading of the
novel, Chal Windzer's education has cut him off
from his tribal roots and heritage because his
education denies "his basic affinity with the
earth. . . ." Larson finds Chal to be "a weak
character, a questionable hero," and declares
that Chal is even more directionless than the
protagonists of later American Indian novels.
Larson declares *Sundown* to be "the most
accomplished of the novels written by Native
Americans exploring the assimilationist theme,
the most significant early account of the clash
of cultures."

Oaks, Priscilla. "The First Generation of
    Native American Novelists." *MELUS* 5:1,
    (Spring 1978), 57-65.
According to Oaks, the Osage in Mathews' novel
"are torn from their tradition by greed and
materialism." Oaks finds the primary theme of
the novel to be the destructive effects of white
materialism on Indian society, and states that
"The novel depicts the destruction of the tribal
community when oil brings riches to the tribe and
takes away the cohesiveness of a commonly shared
property."

Oaks, Priscilla. Introduction to *Sundown*.
Boston: Gregg Press, 1979, v-xi.
In this brief introduction to the 1979 reprint of
Mathews' novel, Oaks provides historical background concerning the period of Osage history
dealt with in the novel, concluding that the
wealth brought to the Osage people by oil rights
"made them all very rich and ruined them as human
beings." In a critical analysis echoing her
earlier essay, "The First Generation of Native
American Novelists," Oaks declares that *Sundown*
demonstrates "how wealth did not free the Osages
from oppression and cultural disintegration, but
hastened the process." In developing his protagonist in the slow-paced novel, Mathews is
interested not "in a complicated story but in
character development, specifically Chal's adult
lack of maturity due to his inability to cope
with the pressures of his double cultural birth-
right."

Schneider, Jack. "The New Indian: Alienation
and the Rise of the Indian Novel." *South
Dakota Review*, 17 (Winter 1979-80), 67-76.
Schneider surveys fifteen novels about American
Indians and finds that "Indian fiction reveals a
gallery of the dispossessed" who are caught
between worlds and cultures, "too red for the one
and too white for the other." He finds the
central dilemma for the protagonist of Indian
fiction to be that of acculturation, and declares
that *Sundown* reveals "that hundreds of years of
racial conditioning stand between the educated
Indian and his aspirations of walking the White
Man's Road." Schneider stresses Chal Windzer's
"humiliating awareness that he is a misfit among
the whites . . . ."

Reviews of *Sundown*

Books. December 2, 1934, 4.
Christian Science Monitor. November 8, 1934,
18.

New York Times. November 25, 1934, 19.
Saturday Review of Literature. Volume 11,
November 24, 1934, 309.

Biographical Sources

Bailey, Garrick. "John Joseph Mathews: Osage,
1894 -." *American Indian Intellectuals,*
1976 Proceedings of the American
Ethnological Society, ed. by Robert F.
Spencer, Margot Liberty. New York: West
Publishing Co., 1976.
*Literature By and About the American Indian:
An Annotated Bibliography,* ed. by Anna Lee
Stensland. Urbana, Illinois, National
Council of Teachers of English, 1979.

N. Scott Momaday
(1934 -)

I.   **Biography**

Momaday, Kiowa and Cherokee, was born in Lawton,
Oklahoma, and spent most of his youth in the
Southwest. He has B.A., M.A., and Ph.D. degrees
and has taught at several universities, including
the University of California at Santa Barbara,
the University of California at Berkeley, and
Stanford University. Momaday is currently
Professor of English at the University of
Arizona. Momaday has been awarded a John Jay
Whitney Foundation Fellowship, a Guggenheim
Fellowship, and a Fulbright Fellowship, and in
1969 he received a Pulitzer Prize for his novel,
House Made of Dawn.

II. **Primary Sources**

Novels

>   *House Made of Dawn.* New York: Harper and Row,
>   1968. Paperback reprint from New York:
>   Signet Books, 1969.

Abel returns from World War II and finds himself
alienated from the harmonious world of the Southwest Pueblo where he grew up. Drunken and unable
to articulate his feelings, Abel murders a mys-
teriously evil albino and is sent to prison for
six years. Once out of prison, Abel is relocated
in the urban world of Los Angeles where he becomes marginally involved with the Holiness Pan-
Indian Rescue Mission's peyote rituals and fights
against a second sinister force in the form of a
corrupt policeman who leaves Abel beaten and
nearly dead on the beach. In the end, Abel returns to the pueblo and is able to reintegrate
himself into the Indian world of his grandfather
as he takes his grandfather's place with the
runners "running after evil." The novel is

circular in structure, beginning and ending with
the running, and is told in a chronologically
disordered pattern involving stream-of-
consciousness and flashback techniques.

Other Booklength Works

*The Complete Poems of Frederick Goddard
    Tuckerman.* New York: Oxford University
    Press, 1965.
The Journey of Tai-me. Santa Barbara:
    privately printed, 1967.
The Way to Rainy Mountain. Albuquerque:
    University of New Mexico Press, 1969.
    Paper reprint New York: Ballantine, 1970.
Angle of Geese and Other Poems. Boston:
    David. R. Godine. 1974.
The Gourd Dancer. New York: Harper and Row,
    1976.
The Names: A Memoir. New York: Harper and
    Row, 1976.

Selected Shorter Publications

Poems

"Angle of Geese." *New Mexico Quarterly*, 38;
    (Spring 1968), 105. Reprinted in *Quest for
    Reality.* Yvor Winters and Kenneth Fields,
    eds. Chicago: Swallow Press, 1969, 189; in
    Forgotten Pages of American Literature.
    Gerald W. Haslan, ed. Boston: Houghton
    Mifflin Co., 1970, 59; in *Literature of the
    American Indian.* Thomas E. Sanders and
    Walter W. Peek, eds. New York: Glencoe
    Press, 1973, 461; in *Voices From Wah'Kon-
    Tah: Contemporary Poetry of Native
    Americans.* Robert K. Dodge and Joseph B.
    McCullough, eds. New York: International
    Publishers, 1974, 73; and in *Carriers of
    the Dream Wheel: Contemporary Native
    American Poetry.* Duane Niatum, ed. New
    York: Harper & Row Publishers, 1975, 106.

"The Bear." *New Mexico Quarterly*, 31; (Spring 1961), 46. Reprinted in *New Mexico Quarterly*, 38; (Spring 1968), 104; in *Speaking for Ourselves: American Ethnic Writing*. Lillian Faderman and Barbara Bradshaw, eds. Glenview, Illinois: Scott, Foresman & Co., 1969, 515; in *The Range of Literature*, 3rd Edition. Elisabeth W. Schneider, Albert L. Walker, and Herbert G. Childs, eds. New York: D. Van Nostrand, 1973, 487; in Dodge and McCullough, *Voices from Wah'Kon-tah*, 72; and in Niatum, *Carriers of the Dream Wheel*, 91.

"The Bear and the Colt." In Faderman and Bradshaw, *Speaking for Ourselves*, 472-76.

Before an Old Painting of the Crucifixion." *Southern Review*, 1; (Spring 1965), 421-23. Reprinted in *New Mexico Quarterly*, 38; (Spring 1968), 106-107; in Winters and Fields, *Quest for Reality*, 191-193; in Haslan, *Forgotten Pages of American Literature*, 58-59; and in Sanders and Peek, *Literature of the American Indian*, 462.

"Blue." (from "The Colors of Night.") In *Bear Crossings*. Anne Newman and Julie Suk, eds. Newport Beach, California: The New South Co., 37.

"The Burning." *Pembroke Magazine*. No. 6, (1975), 31.

"But Then and There the Sun Bore Down." In Niatum, *Carriers of the Dream Wheel*, 105.

"Buteo Regalis." *New Mexico Quarterly*, 31; (Spring 1961), 47. Reprinted in *New Mexico Quarterly*, 38; (Spring 1968), 104; in Faderman and Bradshaw, *Speaking for Ourselves*, 515; and in Dodge and McCullough, *Voices from Wah'Kon-tah*, 77.

"Carriers of the Dream Wheel." In Niatum, *Carriers of the Dream Wheel*, 87.

"The Colors of Night." In *Songs From This Earth on Turtle's Back: Contemporary American Indian Poetry*. Joseph Bruchac, ed. Greenfield Center, New York: The Greenfield Review Press, 1983, 158-160.

"The Delight Song of Tsoai-Talee." In Niatum,
  Carriers of the Dream Wheel, 89. Reprinted
  in Bruchac, *Songs From This Earth on
  Turtle's Back*, 158.
"The Eagle-Feather Fan." In Niatum, *Carriers
  of the Dream Wheel*, 98.
"The Eagles of Valle Grande." In Faderman and
  Bradshaw, *Speaking for Ourselves*, 476-481.
"Earth and I Gave You Turquoise." *New Mexico
  Quarterly*, 29; (Summer 1959), 156.
  Reprinted in *New Mexico Quarterly*, 38;
  (Spring 1968), 103; in *From the Belly of
  the Shark: A New Anthology of Native
  Americans*. Walter Lowenfels, ed. New York:
  Vintage Books, 1973, 44; in Dodge and
  McCullough, *Voices from Wah'Kon-tah*, 74; in
  Niatum, *Carriers of the Dream Wheel*, in
  Understanding Poetry, 4th Edition. Cleanth
  Brooks and Robert Penn Warren, eds. New
  York: Holt, Rinehardt and Winston, 1976,
  436; and in *Earth Air Fire and Water*,
  Francis Monson McCullogh, ed. New York:
  Coward, McCann, and Geoghegan, 1971, 59.
"The Fear of Bo-talee." In Bruchac, *Songs From
  This Earth on Turtle's Back*, 160. Reprinted
  in *The Remembered Earth: An Anthology of
  Contemporary Native American Literature*.
  Geary Hobson, ed. Albuquerque, N.M.: Red
  Earth Press, 1979, 174.
"For The Old Man Mad for Drawing, Dead at
  Eighty-Nine." *Pembroke Magazine*. No. 6
  (1975), 31.
"Forms of the Earth at Abiquiv." In Niatum,
  Carriers of the Dream Wheel, 88.
"The Gourd Dancer." In Niatum, *Carriers of the
  Dream World*, 94-95. Reprinted in Hobson,
  The Remembered Earth, 175-176, and in
  Bruchac, *Songs From This Earth on Turtle's
  Back*, 161-162.
"The Great American Poem." *Antaeus*, 32;
  (Winter 1979), 82-86.
"Headwaters." In Hobson, *The Remembered Earth*,
  173.

"The Horse That Died of Shame." In Hobson, *The
Remembered Earth*, 174.
"Krasnopresnenskaya Station." In Hobson, *The
Remembered Earth*, 176.
"Los Alamos." *New Mexico Quarterly*, 29;
(Autumn 1959), 306.
"Pit Viper." *New Mexico Quarterly*, 31; (Spring
1961), 47. Reprinted in *New Mexico
Quarterly*, 38; (Spring 1968), 102; in Dodge
and McCullough, *Voices from Wah'Kon-tah*,
76; and in Niatum, *Carriers of The Dream
Wheel*, 100.
"Plainview: 3." In Niatum, *Carriers of the
Dream Wheel*, 103.
"Rainy Mountain Cemetery." *New Mexico
Quarterly*, 38; (Spring 1968), 107.
Reprinted in Hobson, *The Remembered Earth*,
173, and in Niatum, *Carriers of the Dream
Wheel*, 99.
"Simile." *New Mexico Quarterly*, 38; (Spring
1968), 108. Reprinted in Niatum, *Carriers
of the Dream Wheel*, 101.
"The Story of the Well-Made Shield." In
Hobson, *The Remembered Earth*, 174.
Reprinted in Niatum, *Carriers of the Dream
Wheel*, 104.
"To a Child Running With Outstretched Arms in
Canyon de Chelly." In Niatum, *Carriers of
the Dream Wheel*, 92.
"Trees and Evening Sky." In Niatum, *Carriers
of the Dream Wheel*, 102.
"Wide Empty Landscape With a Death in the
Foreground." In Niatum, *Carriers of the
Dream Wheel*, 90.
"Winter Holding Off the Coast of North
America." In Niatum, *Carriers of the Dream
Wheel*, 93.

Short Fiction

"The Bear and the Colt." In *American Indian
Authors*. Natachee Scott Momaday, ed.
Boston: Houghton Mifflin Co., 1972, 119-
124.

"From *The Way To Rainy Mountain.*" In Momaday,
American Indian Authors, 125-131.
"July 20" (excerpt from *House Made of Dawn*).
In Haslam, *Forgotten Pages of American
Literature,* 61-64.
"Prologue" (excerpt from *House Made of Dawn*).
In Haslam, *Forgotten Pages of American
Literature,* 60.
"Tsoai and the Shieldmaker." *Four Winds,* 1
(Summer 1980), 34-43.

Articles and Essays

"An American Land Ethic." In *Ecotactics: The
Sierra Club Handbook for Environmental
Activities.* John G. Mitchell and Constance
L. Stallings, eds. New York: Pocket Books,
1970.
"A Special Sense of Place." *Viva, Santa Fe New
Mexican* (May 7, 1972), 2.
"Indian Facts and Artifacts." *New York Times
Book Review,* 83; (April 30), 1978, 42.
"The Man Made of Words" (from *Indian Voices:
The First Convocation of American Indian
Scholars*). In *Indian Voices.* Jeannette
Henry, ed. San Francisco: Indian Historian,
1973, 49-84. Reprinted in *Literature of the
American Indians: Views and Interpreta-
tions.* Abraham Chapman, ed. New York and
Scarborough, Ontario: The New American
Library, 1975, 96-110, and in *The Remember-
ed Earth: An Anthology of Contemporary
Native American Literature.* Geary Hobson,
ed. Albuquerque, N.M.: Red Earth Press,
1979, 162-172.
"The Morality of Indian Hating." *Ramparts,* 3;
(1964), 30-34.
"Native Amerian Attitudes to the Environment."
In *Seeing With a Native Eye: Essays On
Native American Religion.* Walter Holden
Capps. ed. New York: Harper & Row, 1976,
79-85.

"Now That the Buffalos Gone." *Natural History*,
92; (January 1983), 80.
"Review of Leslie Marmon Silko's *Ceremony*."
New York Times, May 24, 1981.
"Vision Beyond Time and Place." *Life*, 71;
(July 2, 1971), 66-67.

Films

House Made of Dawn. Dir. Larry Littlebird. New
York: New Line Cinema (distributor).

Interviews

"An Interview with N. Scott Momaday." *Puerto
del Sol*, 12; (1973), 33.
"A Conversation with N. Scott Momaday." *Sun
Tracks*, 2:2 (1976), 8-21.
"Interview with Momaday." *S.A.I.L.*, 4:4
(Winter 1980), 1-3.

III. Selected Secondary Sources

Criticism of *House Made of Dawn*

Allen, Paula Gunn. "A Stranger in My Own
Life: Alienation in American Indian Prose
and Poetry." *MELUS* 7:2 (Summer 1980), 3-19.
Allen suggests that a preoccupation with the process of alienation is central to contemporary
American Indian writing. In a discussion of such
writers as Momaday, James Welch, and Leslie
Silko, Allen finds that alienation is characteristic of the life of the Indian "half or mixed
blood." She asserts that Abel, in *House Made of
Dawn*, is an outsider in his pueblo even before
his experience of war, and that in murdering the
albino, "Abel tries to murder that alien other
which he cannot accept and integrate within his
own psyche . . . ."

Barry, Nora Baker. "The Bear's Son Folk Tale
    in *When Legends Die* and *House Made of
    Dawn.*" *Western American Literature*, 12
    (1978), 375-87.
This article traces elements of and parallels to
the Bear's Son tale in both novels. Barry
details the major motifs in European and Asian
folktales of the Bear's Son type and finds that
in *House Made of Dawn*, Abel is "associated with
the Bear's Son type in a subtle and less easily
schematized way than Hal Borland's [*Legends*]
hero." Barry documents elements in the novel
which associate Abel with the Bear's Son type and
finds that these elements make Abel a "universal
hero."

Beidler, Peter G. "Animals and Human
    Development in the Contemporary American
    Indian Novel." *Western American
    Literature*, 14 (Summer 1979), 133-48.
Beidler discusses *House Made of Dawn*, James
Welch's *Winter in the Blood*, and Leslie Silko's
Ceremony, and finds that in all three novels the
protagonist is disoriented by his contact with
the white world and must find "his way back from
confusion to right thinking by attuning himself
with the world of animals." The author traces
Abel's parallels in *House Made of Dawn* to a
succession of animals culminating in Abel's
identification with the bear and eagle on the
reservation, with Abel achieving "the strength
and endurance of the bear" and "the vision of the
eagle."

Brumble, H. David III. "Anthropologists,
    Novelists and Indian Sacred Material." *The
    Canadian Review of American Studies*, 11:1
    (Spring 1980), 31-48.
Brumble explores the awkward position writers
find themselves in when attempting to deal with
Indian sacred materials. The author traces
changing attitudes toward the explication of
Indian sacred materials in this century and

asserts that Momaday "provides the best example
of a writer affected by these concerns." He
suggests that Momaday's "style has, over the
years, changed largely as a response to such
problems." Brumble sees Tosamah's explication of
St. John's text in *House Made of Dawn* as
"Momaday's frank admission of the awkwardness,
and something of the pain of his own situation.
He feels that he must explain to his audience how
to respond to the stories that are so dear to him
. . . ."

Buller, Galen. "New Interpretations of Native
    American Literature: A Survival
    Technique." *American Indian Culture and
    Research Journal*, 4:1-2 (1980), 165-177.
In an overview of American Indian literature,
considering Momaday, Silko, Welch, Niatum and
others, Buller stresses the need for teachers of
Indian literature to recognize that it is
distinct from traditional western literature,
different in "function, style, format, theme and
world-view from post-Renaissance western literature," and that "the contemporary Indian writer
stands with one foot in each of the two literary
traditions." He states that in *House Made of
Dawn*, Abel returns to the restorative land and
that once he is reunited "with his homeland, his
people, and his religion," Abel can realize who
he is and be cured. Ultimately, Buller suggests,
Abel is "a continuation of [his grandfather]
Francisco."

Clements, William M. "Momaday's *House Made of
    Dawn*." *Explicator*, 41:1 (Fall 1982), 60-62.
Clements disagrees with Woodward's thesis in an
earlier *Explicator* essay that Abel imagines the
other runners in the conclusion to *House Made of
Dawn*. Clements insists that Momaday intends for
the final race to be taken as real because the
race takes place at an appropriate time according
to the Jemez ritual calendar and because the race
occurs "in such close juxtaposition with

Francisco's death." He dismisses concern for the
question of whether or not the race will lead to
Abel's death as a matter of little concern in
reading this novel.

    Davis, Jack L. "The Whorf Hypothesis and
        Native American Literature." *South Dakota
        Review*, 14:2 (1976), 59-72.
Davis provides a brief definition of Whorf's
hypothesis of linguistic relativity "which
postulates that one's perception of the world
and, thus, his ways of thinking and behaving are
deeply influenced by the structure of his
language." Davis applies this hypothesis to
Frank Waters' *The Man Who Killed the Deer* and
Momaday's *House Made of Dawn*, and he suggests
that Abel's attempt to see the world as the white
man sees it has rendered him "nearly inarticu-
late" in both white and native tongues.

    Dickinson-Brown, Roger. "The Art and
        Importance of N. Scott Momaday." *The
        Southern Review*, 14 (Winter 1978), 30-45.
Dickinson-Brown calls *House Made of Dawn* "a
memorable failure," and asserts that the novel
falls apart into "a batch of often dazzling
fragments." Dickinson-Brown finds the novel's
ending "evasive," and suggests that the novel's
landscape is its most successful feature. This
critic goes on to praise Momaday's syllabic
poetry highly and to state that Momaday's poem,
"Angle of Geese," is "the best example of
Momaday's greatness."

    Dillingham, Peter. "The Literature of the
        American Indian." *English Journal*, 62:1
        (1973), 37-41.
In this early survey of contemporary Indian
literature, Dillingham praises the poetry of
Momaday and James Welch, mentions Dallas Chief
Eagle's novel, *Winter Count*, and declares that
Momaday's *House Made of Dawn* "is perhaps the
finest piece of writing by an Indian author to

date." Calling the novel "a sensitive portrayal
of the Indian as a stranger in his native land,"
Dillingham recommends the work for older students
and states that "*House Made of Dawn* encompasses
all the major themes to be found in Indian
literature . . . ."

Dorris, Michael. "Native American Literature
    in an Ethnohistorical Context." *College
    English*, 41 (October 1979), 147-161.
Dorris' essay discusses the problems involved in
generalizing in the classroom about "Native
American Literature." Pointing to the cultural
diversity among native inhabitants of North
America, Dorris argues that there is no such
thing as an "Indian literature," but rather a
multitude of Native American literatures. Dorris
suggests that *House Made of Dawn* should not be
taken as literal statement of fact, but as a
product "of artistic imagination and license,"
and further argues that in Momaday's novel Abel
"is not the product of his background (and
therefore 'representative'), but he rather moves
through it in his own unique way."

Espey, David B. "Endings in Contemporary
    American Indian Fiction." *Western American
    Literature*, 13 (Summer 1978), 133-139.
Espey considers works by Welch, Silko, and
Momaday, examining attitudes toward death in each
work. He argues that in *House Made of Dawn* Abel
returns in failure to his village at the end of
the novel but that through his act of joining the
dawn runners Abel transcends his fear of death
and is reunited with "his ancestral and cultural
past."

Evers, Lawrence J. "Words and Place: A
    Reading of *House Made of Dawn*." *Western
    American Literature*, 11 (1977), 297-320.
Evers discusses Abel's loss of "sense of place"
in *House Made of Dawn* and reads the novel as an
"emergence narrative" or journey suggestive of

the traditional Navajo emergence narrative
through which "the Navajos determined who and
what they were in relation to the land." Evers
sees the novel's conclusion as positive, suggesting that "All signs point to a new beginning
for Abel . . . ."

    Hirsch, Bernard A. "Self-Hatred and Spiritual
       Corruption in *House Made of Dawn*." *Western*
       American Literature, 17:4 (February 1983),
       307-320.
Hirsch focuses on Abel's relationship with three
figures in urban Los Angeles: Martinez, Tosamah,
and Benally. Each of these three, according to
Hirsch, shares the quality of self-contempt, and
"the strong responses Abel generates in each of
these characters indicate their perception of
something unyielding and incorruptible in him,
something which throws into stark relief the
humiliating spiritual compromises they have felt
compelled to make." Abel becomes their scapegoat
because he threatens the illusions they have
fostered to ensure emotional and psychological
survival in Los Angeles. While Martinez uses
violence and fear to control his world, Tosamah
uses language and is compared by Hirsch to
Coyote, a "master of self-deception." Tosamah is
embarrassed by Abel, but Benally sincerely tries
to help Abel while simultaneously trying to sell
himself on the American Dream. Each of these
three characters, Hirsch concludes, "projects his
own diminished sense of self upon Abel and res-
ponds to that self in his own way."

    Hogan, Linda. "Who Puts Together." *Denver*
       Quarterly, 14:4 (1980), 103-112.
Hogan traces the significance of the Navajo Night
Chant ceremony in *House Made of Dawn* and examines
the use of language as a healing power in the
ceremony. She suggests that Momaday merges the
Navajo healing ceremony with Abel's experiences
in order to "restore Abel to his place within the
equilibrium of the universe." As a healing

power, language can restore us to unity with
earth and universe, but it is also capable of un-
doing. Thus, Hogan asserts, Abel is both undone
and healed through the power of the word.

Hunter, Carol. "American Indian Literature."
    MELUS 8:2 (Summer 1981), 82-85.
Hunter divides American Indian literature into
two categories: traditional oral literature and
modern fiction and contends that "American Indian
writers in the 1980's project tribal ethos,
regional identity, and their cultural heritage"
from traditional oral literature. Hunter comments briefly upon Momaday's use of the Kiowa
oral historical calendar in *The Way to
Rainy Mountain* and of Pueblo and Navajo material
in *House Made of Dawn*.

Hylton, Marion Willard. "On a Trail of
    Pollen: Momaday's *House Made of Dawn*."
    Critique, 14:2 (1972), 60-69.
Hylton reads the novel as the story of a man
denied the necessary psychic ties to land and
place and forced into an alien culture. Abel is
a victim of "disharmony and alienation" due in
large part to his affair with the white woman,
Angela. When Abel returns to the village at the
novel's end and takes part in the race, however,
"he becomes a part of the orderly continuum of
interrelated events that constitute the Indian
universe . . . ."

Kerr, Blaine. "The Novel as Sacred Text: N.
    Scott Momaday's Myth-Making Epic."
    Southwest Review, 63:2 (Spring 1978), 172-
    79.
Kerr states that Momaday, in *House Made of Dawn*,
may "be seeking to make the modern Anglo novel a
vehicle for a sacred text." He defines the
novel's concern as "survival, not salvation," and
suggests that Momaday "has mythified Indian
consciousness into a modern novel."

Larson, Charles R. *American Indian Fiction.*
Albuquerque: University of New Mexico
Press, 1978, 78-96.
In his subsection on *House Made of Dawn*, Larson
sees the novel as very pessimistic. He reads the
work as a protest, as "the most searing indict-
ment of the white world by a Native American
novelist," and he finds no hope for Abel or the
American Indian in the novel. Larson defines
Abel's final run as a "run toward death, a kind
of ritual suicide, and not an act of renewal . .
. ."

Lattin, Vernon E. "The Quest for Mythic Vision
in Contemporary Native American and Chicano
Fiction." *American Literature,* 50 (January
1979), 625-640.
Lattin finds in both Chicano and Native American
fiction today "an intense desire to recapture and
restate the sacred vision which physical conquest
has not been able to destroy." He reads *House
Made of Dawn* as a presentation of the failure of
Christianity, finding examples of such failure in
both Father Olguin and Tosamah. In returning to
his pueblo, Abel "unites himself with his sacred
past." Lattin further asserts that Momaday has
helped to create a "new romanticism," which
Lattin defines as "an optimistic fiction with the
protagonist returning to wholeness and mythic
vision and transcending the limitations of both
society and time."

Lincoln, Kenneth. *Native American Renaissance.*
Berkeley, CA: University of California
press, 1983, 117-121.
After providng an overview of Momaday's work,
from *The Gourd Dancer* and *The Journey of Tai-me*
to *The Way to Rainy Mountain* and *The Names,*
Lincoln devotes several pages of his book to a
discussion of *House Made of Dawn.* Lincoln points
out Momaday's incorporation of modern fictional
techniques, including the interior monologue and
multiple time shifts characteristic of Faulkner,

and makes a connection between this novel and
"Lawrence's neoprimitivism." He finds that
"Natural rituals of the body offer Abel regenera-
tion through Pueblo traditions," and that the
"ceremonies promise a reordered life through
childhood visions, remembered vividly . . . ."
The albino of the novel, according to Lincoln, is
"an embodiment of the machine of war," and Angela
Grace St. John "is an angel of condescending
grace" representing empty spirituality and "pre-
datory sexuality." Lincoln reads the novel's
conclusion positively, stating "It is a sunrise
image of reintegration, of renaissance."

   McAllister, Harold S. "Incarnate Grace and the
      Paths of Salvation in *House Made of Dawn*."
      South Dakota Review, 12:4 (1974), 115-25.
Focusing on the role of Angela in the novel,
McAllister stresses her Catholicism and identifies her symbolically with the Virgin Mary. He
details numerous elements of Catholicism in the
novel, including significant dates and names, and
he suggests that the novel might well be a
Christian morality play, with its subject "spiritual redemption in a squalid, hellish temporal
world." According to this critic, Angela is
saved through her contact with the Indians and
her affair with Abel. Simultaneously, Angela
shows Abel the path of salvation.

   McAllister, Harold S. "Be a Man, Be a
      Woman: Androgyny in *House Made of Dawn*."
      American Indian Quarterly, 2 (1976), 14-22.
In this article, McAllister explores the moral
and thematic function of the priest, Father
Nicolás, and finds a connection between Father
Nicolás and the witch and the murdered albino.
The three are "in a complex, magical way, three
manifestations of a single person." McAllister
cites the Pueblo tradition of androgyny as a
postive ideal, a "Jungian balance of male and
female," and he states that Nicolás fails to
"integrate the anima and the animus into a

unified personality" and that he becomes "not
potent male/female but an impotent, emasculated
man, disguised as or even transformed into a
woman: the witch Nicolás."

Oleson, Carole. "The Remembered Earth:
    Momaday's *House Made of Dawn.*" *South
    Dakota Review,* 11:1 (1973), 59-78.
Oleson provides a careful explication of the
novel's structure and concludes that the novel is
"not a short novel about Abel, but a long prose
poem about the earth." The strength in the novel
comes "from changeless change, the unending repe-
tition of the seasonal cycle." Oleson reads the
novel's conclusion as positive; the novel's primary symbols are "dawn, everlasting earth, and
runners able to outlast their pain--all symbols
of hope which contain a prophecy of the Indian
culture's prevailing ultimately."

Ortiz, Simon J. "Towards a National Indian
    Literature: Cultural Authenticity in
    Nationalism." *MELUS* 8:2 (Summer 1981), 7-
    12.
Ortiz suggests that by incorporating non-Indian
religions and languages, American Indians "have
creatively responded to forced colonization." He
defines this creative response as a form of
resistance on the part of American Indians.
According to Ortiz, Abel, in *House Made of Dawn,*
struggles "not only for identity and survival,
but, more, to keep integral what is most precious
to him: the spiritual knowledge which will guide
him throughout his life as it has guided those
before him." Ortiz reads the novel's conclusion
as positive: "Momaday concludes his novel by the
affirmation that dawn will always come and renewal of life will be possible through resistance
against forces which would destroy life."

Robinson, David. "Angles of Vision in N. Scott
    Momaday's *House Made of Dawn.*" *Essays
    on Minority Culture.* Selected Proceedings

of the 3rd Annual Conference on Minority
Studies, volume 2, eds. George E. Carter
and James R. Parker. La Crosse:
University of Wisconsin, 1976, 129-141.
Robinson examines the different perspectives
offered in the novel and compares it to
Faulkner's *The Sound and the Fury* and *As I Lay
Dying* because of its "fragmented viewpoint."
Robinson suggests that Momaday used the fragmented viewpoint to solve the problem of "transla-
ting" an "experience, a tradition, and a world
view fundamentally different from that of most of
his audience."

　　Rosen, Kenneth. "American Indian Literature:
　　　　Current Condition and Suggested Research."
　　　　*American Indian Culture and Research
　　　　Journal*, 3:2 (1979), 57-66.
In an essay surveying American Indian fiction,
Rosen finds *House Made of Dawn* to be "a complex,
profound, and sometimes obscure work that reveals
a sophisticated intelligence and finely honed
sensibility attempting to deal with difficult
material." He describes the novel as essentially
traditional, "told in a twentieth century version
of the oral tradition." Abel, according to
Rosen, is "a modern version of one of Dante's
lost souls, an Indian who can't function in the
Anglo world because that world will make few
concessions to myth or tradition. . . ." Rosen
suggests the need for further critical study of
relationships in the novel, particularly those of
Abel and Francisco and Abel and Tosamah.

　　Schneider, Jack. "The New Indian: Alienation
　　　　and the Rise of the Indian Novel." *South
　　　　Dakota Review*, 17 (Winter 1979-80), 67-76.
In a survey of fifteen novels about American
Indians, Schneider finds that "Indian fiction
reveals a gallery of the dispossessed" who are
"cruelly transfixed between two cultures, too red
for the one and too white for the other." He
labels the central dilemma for the Indian to be

that of acculturation, a process which destroys
the Indian world. In describing the extreme
difficulty facing the Indian protagonist in an
urban setting, Rosen states that in *House Made of
Dawn* "the ultimate cause of Abel's suffering was
that he was simply too Indian to be anything
else."

Standiford, Lester A. "Worlds Made of Dawn:
Characteristic Image and Incident in Native
American Imaginative Literature." *Ethnic
Literatures Since 1776: The Many Voices of
America*, Part 2. Proceedings of the
Comparative Literature Symposium, v. IX,
eds. Wolodymyr T. Zyla and Wendell M.
Aycock. Lubbock: Texas Tech Press, 1978,
327-52.
Standiford argues that contemporary American
Indian literature must be considered by critics
as a hybrid form, one requiring knowledge of both
Indian and Anglo-American traditions. He
stresses the need for critics to be aware of
characteristics distinguishing Indian literature
from the mainstream of Anglo-American literature.
Standiford dates the founding of a "contemporary
imaginative literature" from Momaday's Pulitzer
Prize for *House Made of Dawn* in 1969, and he
argues that critics unaware of the crucial distinctions between Indian writing and mainstream
literature have "made serious errors in discussing such works as Momaday's *House Made of Dawn*."

Stensland, Anna Lee. "Indian Literature and
the Adolescent." *Identity and Awareness in
the Minority Experience*. Selected
Proceedings of the 1st and 2nd Annual
Conferences on Minority Studies. La
Crosse: University of Wisconsin, 1975, 138-
54.
Stensland discusses the dearth of serious study
of Indian literature in adolescent classrooms and
offers suggested approaches to Indian literature
for both junior and senior high school students.

She recommends *House Made of Dawn* for senior
students, commenting on the novel's "hazy plot
line and a well-known hero type, the angry young
man who finds solace in alcohol, drugs, and
sex." It is the fact that Abel is a recognizable
"type" to high school students which, according
to Stensland, "makes possible the teaching of the
book at all." Without such familiarity, she
suggests, the student reader would be lost.

    Strelke, Barbara. "N. Scott Momaday: Racial
       Memory and Individual Imagination."
       *Literature of the American Indians: Views
       and Interpretations,* ed. with introduction
       and notes by Abraham Chapman. New York:
       New American Library, 1975, 348-57.
Strelke suggests that in *House Made of Dawn*
Momaday blends "elements of western philosophy
and literature with specific aspects of Indian
culture and art." She identifies Abel's *"angst"*
as a western element in the novel, while the art,
song, and poetry in the book are Indian along
with the nature imagery and the novel's four-part
structure. She points to Abel's place between
Indian and white cultures and states that "At the
end of the novel Abel cures himself by experiences and learning from the two cultures in which
he lives."

    Trimble, Martha Scott. *N. Scott Momaday.*
       Western Writers Series, No. 9. Boise,
       Idaho: Boise State College, 1973, 1826.
In this general introduction to Momaday and his
writing, Trimble provides a summary of *House Made
of Dawn,* stressing the novel's circular structure
and shifting point-of-view. She finds that
Momaday, in presenting the difficult range of
relationships between Indian and white cultures
"wishes to leave at least the non-Indian reader
with an abiding sense of what he does not know."
She asserts that the novel "is a complex, symbolic expression of how language and culture tend
through their own territorial imperatives to en-
compass one, sometimes to a point of isolation."

Trimmer, Joseph F. "Native Americans and the
American Mix: N. Scott Momaday's *House
Made of Dawn*." *Indiana Social Studies
Quarterly*, 28 (1975), 75-91.
Trimmer provides a close scrutiny of the major
characters and scenes in the novel and states
that "the novel warns native Americans that they
may lose more than they gain if they assimilate
into the American mix." The American culture as
represented in the novel is distempered and
dangerous, and "Abel chooses the Indian culture
because its rituals, traditions, and ways of
perceiving offer a more wholesome and sustaining
vision of manners and manhood."

Velie, Alan R. "Cain and Abel in N. Scott
Momaday's *House Made of Dawn*." *Journal
of the West*, 17:2 (April 1978), 55-62.
Velie argues here that it is a mistake to see
Abel in this novel as a "noble red victim of the
barbaric forces of white America." He stresses
Abel's biblical namesake as an indicator that
Abel is the archetypal victim and contends that
those who do the worst damage to Abel are (like
Cain) his brother Indians: Fragua, the albino,
and Tosamah, the Priest of the Sun.

Velie, Alan R. "*House Made of Dawn*: Nobody's
Protest Novel." *Four American Indian
Literary Masters*. Norman: University of
Oklahoma Press, 1982, 52-64.
In his chapter on *House Made of Dawn* from this
book on Momaday, Silko, Welch, and Vizenor, Velie
repeats his argument from the earlier article in
Journal of the West. He states that it is sim-
plistic to read *House Made of Dawn* as a protest
novel and points out that Abel's difficulties
"stem chiefly from the intolerance of other
Indians." In the end, according to Velie, Abel
is able to return to the pueblo and integrate
himself into the Tanoan culture he had left. But
Velie stresses that Abel has not rejected white
culture in favor of his Indian past; Velie sug-

gests that the two cultures coexist: "There is
no such thing as a pure culture."

Waniek, Marilyn Nelson. "The Power of Language
   in N. Scott Momaday's *House Made of Dawn*."
   Minority Voices, 4:1 (1980), 23-28.
Waniek declares that "the power of language is an
important theme in *House Made of Dawn*." Drawing
upon Ernest Cassirer's *Language and Myth*, Waniek
finds a distinction in the novel between "the
language of logic and the language of myth," the
language of logic belonging to the white world
and the language of myth to the Indian. Each of
the novel's six major characters, Waniek suggests, represents "in varying degrees the power
of language." This critic then goes on to examine the relationship of each character to language, or the word, and to conclude that in the
end Abel has learned from Francisco and other
characters in the novel "the power of language to
create and to heal."

Watkins, Floyd C. "Culture Versus Anonymity in
   House Made of Dawn." In *Time and Place:
   Some Origins of American Fiction*. Athens:
   The University of Georgia Press, 1977, 133-
   171.
Watkins' chapter on *House Made of Dawn* combines
explication of the novel with details concerning
the Jemez pueblo where the novel is set and
information about Southwest Indians in general.
Watkins calls the novel "one of the finest recent
novels in America," and describes it as a work
"about man's loss of tradition, past, community,
nature, fellow man, religion, even meaning." He
states that the novel "treats an older scheme of
things, an ancient natural and supernatural
vision of evil, good, and the world."

Woodard, Charles L. "Momaday's *House Made of
   Dawn*." *Explicator*, 36:2 (Winter 1978), 27-
   28.

In a unique reading, Woodard suggests that at the
novel's conclusion Abel goes into the dawn alone
and runs while "imagining the other runners."
According to Woodard, "This reading eradicates
any traces of contrivance [by Momaday], and it
gives the ending a lyric intensity."

　　Zachrau, Thekla. "N. Scott Momaday: Towards
　　　　An Indian Identity." *Dutch Quarterly Review
　　　　of Anglo-American Letters*, 9 (1979), 52-70.
Zachrau discusses *House Made of Dawn, The Way
to Rainy Mountain,* and *The Names.* She explores
the theme of alienation in *House Made of Dawn* in
its different forms: feeling of powerlessness,
meaninglessness, cultural estrangement, social
isolation, self-alienation. The essay looks
closely at Momaday's narrative technique and
finds that Momaday endangers the organic unity of
his novel by forcing the reader to retrace the
literary technique "in order to stay clear-
sighted." Zachrau finds the solution offered by
the novel to be romanticized, that Abel regains
Eden simply by returning to the world of his
grandfather. Zachrau states, "This conclusion
comes dangerously near the Rousseauistic ideology
of the nobel savage and the wholesome return to
nature."

Reviews of *House Made of Dawn*

　　Atlantic. Volume 222, July 1968, 106.
　　Best Sellers. Volume 28, June 15, 1968, 131.
　　Commonweal. Volume 88, September 20, 1968,
　　　　636.
　　Educational Leadership. Volume 31, April 1974,
　　　　593.
　　English Journal. Volume 63, December 1974, 93.
　　Library Journal. Volume 93, June 15, 1968,
　　　　2522.
　　Listener. Volume 81, May 15, 1969, 686.
　　Nation. Volume 207, August 5, 1968, 91.
　　Natural History. Volume 79, June 1970, 78.
　　New Statesman. Volume 77, May 16, 1969, 696.

New York Times Book Review. June 9, 1968, 5.
New York Times Book Review. August 9, 1970,
    27.
New York Times Book Review. October 9, 1977,
    45.
Observer (London). May 25, 1969, 26.
Publishers Weekly. Volume 196, September 22,
    1969, 86.
Southern Review. Volume 14, January 1978, 30.
Spectator. Volume 222, May 23, 1969, 687.
Times Literary Supplement. May 22, 1969, 549.
Village Voice. Volume 15, January 29, 1970, 8.

Biographical Sources

*American Authors and Books, 1640 to the
    Present Day.* 3rd Edition. Ed. by W.J. Burke
    and Will D. Howe. Revised by Irving Weiss
    and Anne Weiss. New York: Crown Publishing,
    Inc., 1972.
Best Sellers. June 15, 1968.
Childhood in Poetry. Supplement 1, vol. 2. Ed.
    by John MacKay Shaw. Detroit: Gale Research
    Co., 1972.
Commonweal. Sept. 20, 1968.
Contemporary American Indian Leaders. Ed. by
    Marion E. Bridley. New York: Dodd, Mead &
    Co., 1972.
Contemporary Authors. vol. 25, Detroit: Gale
    Research Co., 1971.
Contemporary Literary Criticism. vol. 2.
    Detroit: Gale Research Co., 1976.
Contemporary Novelists. 2nd Edition. Ed. by
    James Vinson and D.L. Kirpatrick. New York:
    St. Martin's Press, 1976.
Contemporary Novelists. 3rd Edition. Ed. by
    D.L. Kirpatrick. New York: St. Martin's
    Press, 1982.
Current Bibliography. vol. 36. April 1975.
A Directory of American Fiction Writers. New
    York: Poets and Writers, Inc., 1976.
Directory of American Scholars. 6th Edition,
    vol. 2. Ed. by Jaques Cattell Press. New
    York: R.R. Bowker Co., 1974.

Forgotten Pages of American Literature. Gerald
W. Haslen, ed. Boston: Houghton Mifflin
Co., 1970.
Forms of Discovery, ed. by Yvor Winter.
Chicago: Swallow Press, 1967.
Indian of Today. Marion E. Bridley, ed.
I.C.F.P. Inc., 1971.
The Nation. August 5, 1968.
Natural History. vol. 84, no. 2. February
1975.
New York Times. May 6, 1969.
New York Times Magazine. Dec. 27, 1981.
New York Times Book Review. June 9, 1968.
Saturday Review. June 21, 1969.
Something About the Author. vol. 30. Detroit:
Gale Research Co., 1978.
Voices from Wah'Kon-tah. Ed. by Robert K.
Dodge & Joseph B. McCullough. New York:
International Publishers, 1974.
Washington Post. Nov. 21, 1969.
Who's Who in America. 38th Edition, vol. 2.
Chicago: Marquis' Who's Who, 1974.
The Writer's Directory. New York: St. Martin's
Press, 1976.

Nasnaga (Roger Russell)
(1941 -)

I. Biography

Nasnaga, a member of the Shawnee tribe, is an
artist and a draftsman.

II. Primary Sources

Novels

  Indians' Summer. New York: Harper and Row,
  1975.
The Navajo, Sioux, Mohawk, Apache, and Pueblo
nations declare their independence from the
United States on July 4, 1976, upsetting the
American President's plans for bicentennial
festivities. The Indians seize National Guard
equipment and munitions and seal off large parts
of New Mexico, Oklahoma, South Dakota, and the
Quebec-New York border and, aided by the nation
of India, they gain recognition by the United
Nations and the support of Russia, China, and
Third World countries. The Indians aim three
Minuteman nuclear missles at Washington, and
after a few skirmishes, win their bluffing
contest with the Pentagon.

III. Selected Secondary Sources

Criticism of *Indians' Summer*

  Larson, Charles R. *American Indian Fiction*.
    Albuquerque: University of New Mexico
    Press, 1978, p. 161-64.
In his brief treatment of this novel, Larson
labels it a "satirical spoof" and states that
"Largely because the author has taken a one-gag
idea and stretched it out for nearly two hundred
pages, the humor quickly collapses." However, in

spite of his criticism, Larson calls *Indians'
Summer* "a novel that touches several of the more
important themes and issues from earlier fiction
by Native Americans" and points to the theme of
Pan-Indianism in Nasnaga's work.

> Rosen, Kenneth. "American Indian Literature:
> Current Condition and Suggested Research."
> *American Indian Culture and Research
> Journal*, 3 (1979), p. 57-66.

In this essay surveying contemporary American
Indian literature, Rosen comments briefly on
Indians' Summer, calling the novel's humor
"rather strained" and stating that "the story
suffers from imagery apparently arrested in its
1973 Wounded Knee stage of development." Like
Larson, Rosen points to the Pan-Indianism as a
postive element in the novel and concludes that
the work "had the virtue of considering traditional tribal unity as the indivisible core of
whatever it is that will eventually mean survival
for Native American people."

Reviews of *Indians' Summer*

> *American Indian Quarterly*. Volume 2, Winter
> 1974-75, p. 294.
> *Booklist*. Volume 71, June 15, 1975, p. 1071.
> *Christian Science Monitor*. Volume 67, March
> 26, 1975, p. 9.
> *English Journal*. Volume 65, January 1976, p.
> 96.
> *Library Journal*. Volume 100, May 1, 1975, p.
> 882.
> *New Republic*. Volume 172, March 29, 1975, p.
> 33.
> *Virgina Quarterly Review*. Volume 51, Summer
> 1975, p. R124.

John Milton Oskison
(1874 - 1947)

I. **Biography**

Oskison, a member of the Cherokee tribe, was born
at Vinita, in Indian Territory. Oskison received
a B.A. from Stanford University, where he began
publishing short fiction in the *Stanford Sequoia*
as well as contributing fiction and nonfiction
pieces to his hometown newspaper, the Vinita
Indian Chieftain. After graduating from
Stanford, Oskison did graduate work at Harvard
before beginning a career in journalism. During
his long career, Oskison published three novels
as well as booklength nonfiction works and held
positions with such publications as the New York
Evening Post and *Collier's*. He published widely
in a diverse range of periodicals including
McClure's, *Century Magazine*, *Native American*, *Red
Man*, *Forum*, *Worker's World* and others. Although
Oskison's novels treat Indian characters only
marginally, Oskison's shorter publications demonstrate a lifelong interest in Indian causes and
Indian people.

II. **Primary Sources**

Novels

> *Wild Harvest*. New York: D. Appleton and Co.,
> 1925. Reprint Chicago: White House Book
> Club, 1925.

Set in the Cherokee Nation, this novel tells the
story of Tim Winger's courtship of Nan Forest,
Nan's father's incarceration for shooting a
rustler, and the colorful life of the time in
Indian Territory. Indians figure only marginally
in the novel, with Oskison stressing the civiliz-
ing role of white settlers and the necessity for
Indians to take up farming and ranching like
their white neighbors.

Black Jack Davy. New York: D. Appleton and
   Co., 1926.
Black Jack Davy is nineteen years old when he
comes to the Indian Territory of Oklahoma with
his adopted father and mother, Jim and Mirabelle
Dawes. The family rents a farm from Ned Warrior,
a Cherokee outlaw, and soon is involved in a
battle for the land with a neighboring white
rancher who wants to enlarge his own holdings. A
subplot in the novel involves Davy's growing love
for his adopted uncle's daughter, Mary, and his
strong sensual attraction to Ned Warrior's part-
Cherokee wife, Rose.

Brothers Three. New York: Macmillan Co.,
   1935.
Francis Odell settles at Redbud Creek in Indian
Teritory with a part-Cherokee wife and five-
month-old son. The novel tells of Odell's
successful creation of a ranching empire and the
destruction of the empire in the hands of his
sons following his death. Through poor mining
investments and speculation in the stock market,
the sons lose the estate they inherited and at
the novel's end must return to the land to work
the ranch and pay off the mortgage. Like
Oskison's other novels, *Brothers Three* deals only
incidentally with Indian subject matter.

Other Booklength Works

A Texas Titan: The Story of Sam Houston.
   Garden City, New York: Doubleday, Doran
   and Co., 1929.
*Tecumseh and His Times: The Story of a Great
   Indian.* New York: G.P. Putnam's Sons,
   1938.

Selected Shorter Publications

Short Fiction

"An Indian Animal Story." *Indian School
Journal*, 14 (January 1914), 213.
"Apples of the Hespride, Kansas." *Forum*, 51
(March 1914), 391-408.
"A Schoolmaster's Dissipation." *Indian
Chieftain*, (December 23, 1897), 3.
"Diverse Tongues: A Sketch." *Current
Literature*, 49 (September 1910), 343-344.
"Hired Man's Chance." *Collier's*, 51 (August 9,
1913), 24-25.
"I Match You: You Match Me." *Indian Chieftain*,
(May 27, 1897), 1. Reprinted from the
Stanford Sequoia.
"Only the Master Shall Praise." *The Century
Magazine*, 59 (January 1900), 327-335.
"Out of the Night That Covers." *Delineator*, 78
(August 1911), 80.
"Spider and the Fly." *Woman's Home Companion*,
38 (October 1911), 9.
"Tookh Steh's Mistake." *Indian Chieftain*,
(July 22, 1897), 1-2.
"To Younger's Bend." *Frank Leslie's Monthly*,
56 (June 1903), 182-188.
"The Fall of King Chris." *Frank Leslie's
Monthly*, 56 (October 1903), 586-593.
"The Other Partner." *Collier's*, 74 (December
6, 1924), 14-15.
"The Problem of Old Harjo." *Southern Workman*,
36 (April 1907), 235-241.
"The Quality of Mercy: A Story of the Indian
Territory." *Century Magazine*, 68 (June
1904), 178-181.
"The Singing Bird." *Sunset Magazine*, 54 (March
1925), 5-8.
"Walla-Tenaka-Creek." *Collier's*, 51 (July 12,
1913), 16.
"When the Grass Grew Long." *Century Magazine*,
62 (June 1901), 247-250.

"Young Henry and the Old Man." *McClure's*, 31
(June 1908), 237.

Articles and Essays

"A Border Judge and His Court." *Frank Leslie's
Popular Monthly*, 56 (July 1903), 253-258.
"Acquiring a Standard of Value." *Quarterly
Journal of the Society of American Indians*,
2 (January-March 1914), 391-408.
"Address by J.M. Oskison." *Red Man*, 4 (May
1912), 397-398.
"American Creator of the Aluminum Age."
World's Work, 28 (August 1914), 438-445.
"An Apache Problem." *Quarterly Journal of the
Society of American Indians*, 1 (April
1913), 25-29.
"Arizona and Forty Thousand Indians." *Southern
Workman*, 43 (March 1914), 148-156.
"A Trip to Yosemite Valley." *Indian Chieftain*,
August 8, 1895.
"Back-Firing Against Bolshevism." *Outlook*, 122
(July 30, 1919), 510-515.
"Biologist's Quest." *Overland*, 38 (July 1901),
52-57.
"Boosting the Thrift Idea." *Collier's*, 53
(April 4, 1914), 22.
"Carlisle Commencement." *Collier's*, 45 (June
4, 1910), 21-22.
"Carlisle Commencement as Seen by *Collier's
Weekly*." *Red Man*, 3 (September 1910), 18-
22.
"Case of the Western Slope." *Collier's*, 44
(January 15, 1910), 19.
"Chemist Who Became King of an Industry."
World's Work, 28 (July 1914), 310-315.
"Cherokee Migration." *Tahlequah Arrow*, May 31,
1902.
"Competing With the Sharks." *Collier's*, 44
(February 5, 1910), 19-20.
"Cooperative Cost of Living." *Collier's*, 48
(January 27, 1912), 48.

"Farming on a Business Basis." *System,* 23
(April 1913), 379-384.

"Farm, the Thousand, and the Ifs." *Collier's,*
51 (May 24, 1913), 24 and 51 (June 7,
1913), 24.

"From John Paul Jones to Dewey." *World's Work,*
29 (February 1915), 447-469.

"Herbert Hoover: Engineer-Economist-
Organizer." *Industrial Management,* 65
(March 1923), 2-6.

"Hoover Message to Export Manufacturers."
Industrial Management, 65 (March 1923, 131-
135.

"How You Can Help Feed and Clothe the
Belgians." *World's Work,* 29 (January 1915),
275-277.

"In Governing the Indian, Use the Indian."
American Indian Magazine, 5, (January-March
1917), 36-41.

"In Governing the Indian, Use the Indian!"
Case and Comment, 23 (February 1917), 722-
726.

"In Governing the Indian--Use the Indian."
Tomahawk, September 20, 1917.

"Indian Kicking Races." *Outing,* 65 (January
1915), 441-447.

"John Oskison Writes of His Visit in Europe."
Indian Chieftain, August 9, 1900.

"John Smith Borrows $20." *Collier's,* 43
(September 4, 1909), 14.

"Koenig's Discover." *Collier's,* 45 (May 28,
1910), 20-21.

"Lake Mohonk Conference." *Native American,*
November 4, 1905.

"Less Known Edison." *World's Work,* 28 (June
1914), 180-185.

"Lung-Mender for the Lord." *Collier's,* 44
(February 5, 1910), 24.

"Making an Individual of the Indian."
Everybody's Magazine, 16 (June 1907), 723-
733.

"New Farm Pioneers." *Collier's,* 51 (August 1,
1913), 27.

"New Way to Finance the Vacation." *Delineator*,
    83 (August 1913), 10.
"Only the Master Shall Praise." *Century
    Magazine*, 59 (January 1900), 327-335.
"$1,000 on the Farm." *Collier's*, 51 (April 26,
    1913), 24 and 51 (May 3, 1913), 26.
"Other Partner." *Collier's*, 74 (December 6,
    1924), 14-15.
"Remaining Causes of Indian Discontent." *North
    American Review*, 184 (March 1, 1907), 486-
    493.
"Road to Betatakin." *Outing*, 64 (July-August
    1914), 392-409, 606-623.
"Spider and the Fly." *Woman's Home Companion*,
    38 (October 1911), 9.
"The Closing Chapter: Passing of the Old
    Indian." *Indian Leader*, 17 (May 1914), 6-9.
"The Indian in the Professions." *Red Man*, 4
    (January 1912), 201-204.
"The Little Mother of the Pueblos."
    Delineator, 81 (March 1913), 170.
"The Man Who Interfered." *Southern Workman*, 44
    (October 1915), 557-567.
"The New Indian Leadership." *American Indian
    Maggazine*, 5 (April-June 1917), 93-100.
"The Outlook for the Indian." *Southern
    Workman*, 32 (June 1903), 270-273.
"The President and the Indian: Rich
    Opportunity for the Red Man." *Vinita Weekly
    Chieftain*, December 25, 1907.
"The Record of the Naval Conflicts." *World's
    Work*, 29 (January 1915), 345-350.
"What a Modern Sea Fight is Like." *World's
    Work*, 29 (November 1914), 87-91.
"Why Am I an American?" *World's Work*, 29
    (December 1914), 209-213.
"With Apache Deer Hunters in Arizona." *Outing*,
    64 (April-May 1914), 65-78, 150-163.
"Working for Fame." *Frank Leslie's Popular
    Monthly*, 56 (August 1903), 372-382.

III. Selected Secondary Sources

Criticism of *Wild Harvest*

> Larson, Charles R. *American Indian Fiction.*
> Albuquerque: University of New Mexico
> Press, 1978, 46-48.

In a brief discussion of this novel, Larson gives
a plot summary and observes that the plot is, for
the most part, unconvincing. He suggests that
the plot has been "needlessly extended so that
Oskison can create a narrative long enough for a
book." Larson concudes that "artistically, at
least, *Wild Harvest* is the very nadir of Native
American Fiction," and he suggests that the novel
is propaganda for Oklahoma statehood. Finally,
Larson suggests that the few Indian characters in
Wild Harvest are there "to provide a kind of
backdrop of authenticity, as part of the Indian
territory setting."

> Strickland, Arney L. "John Milton Oskison: A
> Writer of the Transitional Period of the
> Oklahoma Indian Territory." *Southwestern
> American Literature,* 2 (Winter 1972), 125-
> 134.

Strickland provides an overview of Oskison's
writings, from his first short story to his
novels and booklength nonfiction works. Noting
the subtitle of *Wild Harvest: A Novel of
Transition Days in Oklahoma,* Strickland declares
that "Each of his books might have such a subtitle, *mutatis mutandis.*" Oskison's purpose in
his fiction, this critic suggests, "was to show
the transition of his era in a larger sense than
merely its effect on the Indian, for his works
show an interest in America in general."
Critically, Strickland sums up Oskison as "a
reasonably competent stylist," but argues that
Oskison's fiction is damaged by digressions,
melodrama and sentimentality, and stereotyped
characterization. Oskison is recommended for
"younger teenaged readers" in particular by this
critic.

Criticism of *Black Jack Davy*

Larson, Charles R. *American Indian Fiction.*
Albuquerque: University of New Mexico
Press, 1978, 49-51.
Larson observes that the few Indian figures in
this novel are more significant than the ones in
Wild Harvest, but he states that "Oskison does
not make much use of the Indian setting of the
story, except for an occasional aside on Indian
'progress'." Referring to both *Black Jack Davy*
and *Wild Harvest*, Larson calls the novels "unconvincing both in plot and character" and suggests
that events in the two novels "border on the
ludicrous, the unbelievable, the cliché. . . ."

Criticism of *Brothers Three*

Larson, Charles R. *American Indian Fiction.*
Albuquerque: University of New Mexico
Press, 1978, 51-55.
Larson declares this, Oskison's final novel, to
be the author's best, "the work of a more mature
artist." He praises the "more believable"
characters in this novel and states that "The
attitude expressed toward the land in *Brothers
Three* is the one truly Indian aspect of the
novel. . . ." Larson points out that the
character of Henry ("Mister") in the novel is
highly autobiographical.

Oaks, Priscilla. "The First Generation of
Native American Novelists." *MELUS*, 5:1
(Spring 1978), 57-65.
In this review of Indian novels of the thirties,
Oaks discusses Oskison's *Brothers Three* and
states that the book "demonstrates the effects of
the assimilation of common American problems."
Oaks asserts that no "special Indian characteristics" are attributed to the central characters
in the novel, but declares that the characters
"retain the Indian love of the land and loyalty
to the tribe (family)."

Reviews

Wild Harvest
  New York Times. September 20, 1925, 22.
  New York Tribune. October 11, 1925, 13.
  Times (London). Literary Supplement, November
    19, 1925, 774.
  Book Review Digest. November, 1925
  Book Review Digest. May, 1941

Black Jack Davy
  New York Times. October 10, 1926, 10.
  Saturday Review of Literature. Volume 3,
    December 25, 1926, 471.
  Times (London). Literary Supplement. December
    23, 1926, 950.
  Saturday Review of Literature, 3. 1926, 471.
  Book Review Digest. February, 1927

Brothers Three
  Booklist. Volume 32, November 1935, 67.
  Books. September 15, 1935, 6.
  Boston Transcript. September 14, 1935, 4.
  Chicago Daily Tribune. September 14, 1935, 14.
  Christian Science Monitor. September 11, 1935,
    11.
  Book Review Digest. October, 1935
  Cleaveland Open Shelf. October 1935, 20.
  Nation. Volume 141, December 25, 1935, 750.
  New Republic. Volume 84, October 23, 1935,
    313.
  New York Post. December 7, 1935, 7.
  New York Times. September 15, 1935, 6.
  Saturday Review of Literature. Volume 12,
    September 14, 1935, 12.
  Springfield Republican. January 5, 1936, 7e.

Biographical Sources

  *American Authors and Books, 1640 to the
    Present Day.* 3rd ed. revised. By W.J. Burke
    and Will D. Howe, revised by Irving Weiss
    and Anne Weiss. New York: Crown Publishers,
    1972.

*A Bibliography of Native American Writings,
1772-1924.* By Daniel F. Littlefield and
James W. Parins. Metuchen, New Jersey:
Scarecrow Press, 1981.

*Dictionary of North American Authors Deceased
before 1950.* Compiled by Stewart Wallace.
Toronto: Ryerson Press, 1951. Reprint,
Detroit: Gale Research Co., 1968.

A History of American Magazines: 1741-1930. 5
vols. By Frank Luther Mott. Cambridge:
Harvard University Press, Belknap Press,
1930-1968.

*Literature By and About the American Indian:
An Annotated Bibliography.* By Anna Lee
Stensland. Urbana, Illinois: National
Council of Teachers of English, 1979.

Cleveland, Agnes Morley. "Three Musketeers of
Southwestern Fiction." *Overland Monthly,* 87
(December 1929).

Chief George Pierre
(1926 -)

I. **Biography**

Born in the state of Washington, on the east side of the Cascade Mountains, Pierre is a member of the Okanogan tribe and has held the position of Chief of the Colville Confederated Tribes of Washington.

II. **Primary Sources**

Novels

Autumn's Bounty. San Antonio: Naylor Co., 1972.
Alphonse, chief of the Okanogan tribe and strong opponent of termination, sets out as a nearly toothless old man to hunt down a cougar which has killed a young girl. Alphonse believes the old cougar may be the mate of a female Alphonse had killed ten years before; he feels remorse for having killed the cat's mate, and he identifies strongly with the old male. In the course of the hunt, Alphonse must fend off rabid coyotes and starvation before finally killing the old cougar. After the rabid coyotes have devoured all but the head of the cougar, Alphonse returns to his village a respected hunter and hero. A subplot in the novel is Alphonse's successful attempts to defeat a movement for termination within the tribe.

Other Booklength Works

American Indian Crisis. San Antonio: Naylor Co., 1971.

III. Selected Secondary Sources

Criticsm of *Autumn's Bounty*

Larson, Charles R. *American Indian Fiction.*
Albuquerque: University of New Mexico
Press, 1978.
Larson summarizes the plot of *Autumn's Bounty* and
notes the novel's similarity to Hemingway's *The
Old Man and the Sea.* According to Larson, the
novel shows that "greed and materialism . . .
destroy the harmony of a people." Larson finds
the question of termination central to the novel
and suggests that the question of termination "is
at base an attitude toward the land, toward
traditional life." He states that Alphonse, the
protagonist, is one-dimensional and that the
conclusion of the novel is "vastly oversimpli-
fied" and finally that "the dramatic effect of
the novel is weakened by a number of artificial
scenes and dialogues."

Rosen, Kenneth. "American Indian Literature:
Current Condition and Suggested
Research." *American Indian
Culture and Research Journal,* 3:2 (1979),
p. 57-66.
In this survey of American Indian literature,
Rosen finds that "the theme of pride and
professional and personal integrity is clearly
the author's focus" in *Autumn's Bounty,* but that
the novel is marred by Pierre's attempt "to do
for his people what Hemingway had done for an old
Cuban fisherman" in *The Old Man and The Sea.*
According to Rosen, "*Autumn's Bounty* would
benefit from some scholarly explication of the
actual historical events out of which it grew."

Simon Pokagon
(1830 - 1899)

I. Biography

Son of Chief Leopold Pokagon of the Pokagon band
of the Potawatomi Indians, Simon Pokagon succeed-
ed his father and two older brothers as leader of
his people. When the Potawatomi were removed
from their homeland and forced to relocate in
Iowa, Kansas, and Oklahoma, Simon Pokagon remain-
ed in Michigan with his father's clan, attending
first the Notre Dame preparatory school in South
Bend and later Oberlin College and the Twinsburg
Institute in Ohio. Although well-educated,
Pokagon never received a college degree. As his
autobiographical novel, *Queen of the Woods*, makes
clear, Pokagon was concerned with the difficulties Indian people faced in adjusting to non-
Indian culture, and he worked actively all his
life to better conditions for Indian people and
record Indian history and culture that might
otherwise disappear.

II. Primary Sources

Novels

O-Gî-Mäw-Kwe Mit-I-Gwä-Kî. Queen of the Woods.
Hartford, Michigan: C.H. Engle, 1899.
Reprint Berrien Springs, Michigan:
Hardscrabble Books, 1972.
Set in the Great Lakes area, this autobiographic-
al novel tells the story of Pokagon (the narrator
of the novel) and his love for both nature and
Lonidaw, his wife. In the course of the novel,
Pokagon courts and marries Lonidaw and they have
two children, both of whom are directly or
indirectly destroyed by the tragic effects of
alcohol and the surrounding white world. Simon
Pokagon uses his own name and that of his wife
for the principal characters in the novel as well

as details from his own life. Written first in
his native Algonquin language and subsequently
translated into English, *Queen of the Woods*
includes many Algonquin-Algaic words and phrases
which Pokagon translates into English in the
text. Pokagon also provides a glossary of
Algonquin terms in the preface to the novel.
This novel contains a brief biography of the
author.

Other Booklength Works

> *The Red Man's Rebuke.* Hartford, Michigan:
>   C.H. Engle, 1893.
> *Algonquin Legends of South Haven.* Hartford,
>   Michigan: C.H. Engle, 1900?.
> *Pottawattomie Book of Genesis. . .Legends
>   of the Creation of Man.* Hartford,
>   Michigan: C.H. Engle, 1901?.

Selected Shorter Publications

> "An Indian Idyll of Love, Sorrow and Death."
>   *Indian's Friend*, 19 (August 1907), 2, 12.
> "An Indian on the Problems of His Race."
>   *Review of Reviews*, 12 (December 1895), 694-
>   695.
> "An Indian's Observations on the Mating of
>   Geese." *Arena*, 16 (July 1896), 245-248.
> "An Indian's Plea." *Red Man*, 15 (October-
>   November 1898), 5,8.
> "Future of the Red Man." *Forum*, 23 (August
>   1897), 698-708.
> "Indian Superstitions and Legends." *Forum*, 25
>   (July 1898), 618-629.
> "The Massacre of Fort Dearborn at Chicago."
>   *Harper's Monthly*, 98 (March 1899), 649-656.
> "Simon Pokagon on Naming the Indians." *Review
>   of Reviews*, 16 (September 1897), 320-321.
> "The Future of the Red Man." *Red Man*, 14
>   (July-August 1897), 1-2.
> "The Pottawatomies in the War of 1812." *Arena*,
>   26 (July 1901), 48-55.

III. Selected Secondary Sources

Criticism of *Queen of the Woods*

Dickason, David H. "Chief Simon Pokagon: The
   Indian Longfellow." *Indiana Magazine of
   History*, 52, (1961), 127-140.
In a comprehensive examination of the novel,
Dickason provides biographical information concerning Pokagon as well as information about the
author's tribal background and the Algonquin
language. In his analysis of the novel, Dickason
points out the awkwardness of "the often trite
phraseology of the romantic-sentimental tradition," but argues that the "intrinsic subject" of
the novel is "original and fresh," labeling the
work "an emotional and at times lyrical rememb-
rance of things past rather than a synthetic,
sterile exercise such as *Hiawatha*."

Larson, Charles R. *American Indian Fiction*.
   Albuquerque: University of New Mexico
   Press, 1978.
Larson finds evidence in *Queen of the Woods* of
Pokagon's "assimilationist beliefs," and states
that this novel established a pattern of assimilationist novels which lasted for roughly the
next thirty-five years." Larson suggests that
without the final sections on the temperance
theme, "the work would . . . be classified as
romance or pastoral, somewhat in the vein of
Chateaubriand's *Atala* . . . ." According to
Larson, the novel's tone is didactic, the language stilted, and dialogue pompous. He calls
Lonidaw, the female protagnoist, "the closest
approximation to the stereotyped image of a Noble
Savage in all of the novels written by Native
Americans. . . ."

Ruoff, A. LaVonne Brown. "Simon Pokagon. *O-
   Gi-Maw-Kwe Mit-I-Gwa-ki. Queen of the
   Woods.*" *American Literary Realism*, 13
   (Autumn 1980), 317-319.

Ruoff points out the novel's resemblance to the
romances of Chateaubriand and Rousseau and goes
on to examine Pokagon's attempts to achieve "the
willing suspension of disbelief." Ruoff suggests
that Pokagon's use of his and his wife's names
for the narrator and heroine, his use of his
family background, his inclusion of Potawatomi
language, and his inclusion of material concerning the Removal and the fight against alcohol all
combine to create realism in the novel.

Biographical Sources

Buechner, Cecelia Bain. *The Pokagons.* Indiana
    Historical Society Publications, vol. 10,
    no. 5 (1933), 279-340.
"Chief Pokagon Dies." Chicago *Inter Ocean*,
    January 29, 1899. Reprinted in Pokagon,
    Queen of the Woods, Appendix, 242.
Flower, B.O. "An Interesting Representative of
    a Vanishing Race." *Arena*, 16 (July 1896),
    240, 248.
Littlefield, Daniel F. Jr. and James W.
    Parins, eds. *A Bibliography of Native
    American Writings, 1772-1924.* Metuchen, New
    Jersey: Scarecrow Press, 1981.

Leslie Marmon Silko
(1948 -)

I. Biography

Silko, Laguna Pueblo, was raised at Old Laguna in
New Mexico. She attended the local BIA school
until the start of the fifth grade, when she
began to commute to Albuquerque to attend
Catholic schools. In 1969 she completed a B.A.
in English at the University of New Mexico, and
began law school in a program intended to provide
Native Americans with their own lawyers. Her
collection of poetry, *Laguna Woman,* appeared in
1974; and several of her prose works were col-
lected that same year in Kenneth Rosen's *The Man
to Send Rain Clouds: Contemporary Stories by
American Indians.* She taught for two years at
Navaho Community College at Tsaile, Arizona, and
then spent two years in Ketchikan, Alaska, where
she wrote *Ceremony.* She returned to teach at her
old university, and in 1978 she accepted a teaching position at the University of Arizona. In
1981 *Storyteller,* a collection of her poems and
stories, was published.

II. Primary Sources

Novels

Ceremony. New York: Viking, 1977. Paperback
    reprint New York: Signet, 1978.
After surviving horrifying experiences in the
Philippines in World War II, and after an extended stay in a Veteran's Administration mental
ward, Tayo--a young halfbreed--returns to the
Laguna Pueblo in New Mexico. Alienated from his
culture and his family, and disoriented and sick-
ened by his experiences in the Pacific, Tayo is
troubled by paralysis of memory, nightmares, and
fragmentation of reality. The traditional
rituals of Ku'oosh, the old medicine man whom

Tayo's grandmother calls in, are ineffective.
Tayo acts out his despair in drunken, violent,
self-destructive ways. The beginning of Tayo's
salvation comes when his people send him to an
old halfbreed Navaho medicine man named Betonie.
The medicine man knows that all that happens is
part of a cycle, part of a prophecy that was set
in motion long ago. He explains to Tayo that
there is a witchcraft at work which causes all
evil things. Betonie takes Tayo through a ceremony designed to cure him and show him his part
in the greater ceremony which will rid the world
of its great curse. Tayo goes into the mountains
to seek his uncle Josiah's Mexican cattle which
have been stolen, and in the mountains Tayo meets
Ts'eh, a beautiful mountain-spirit woman, who
teaches him more about the ceremony. When Tayo
returns to his people he finds that witchery is
leading his friends Harley, Emo, Leroy, and
Pinkie toward evil. Tayo keeps out of the reach
of the witchery, and his friends turn on one
another. Watching his friends destroy each other
finally causes Tayo to accept that the prophecy
is terrifyingly real. After carrying out his
part in the ceremony, Tayo is accepted into the
tribe and is received into the kiva.

Other Booklength Works

   Laguna Woman: Poems by Leslie Silko.
      Greenfield Center, New York: Greenfield
      Review Press, 1974.
   Storyteller. New York: Viking, 1981.

Selected Shorter Publications

Poems

   "A Hunting Story." A: A Journal of
      Contemporary Literature, 1:1 (Fall 1976),
      11-13. Reprinted in *The First Skin Around
      Me: Contemporary American Tribal Poetry.*
      James L. White, ed. Moorehead, Minnesota:

The Territorial Press, 1976, 72-75, and in
Storyteller. Leslie Marmon Silko. New York:
Viking, 1981, 81.
"Alaskan Mountain Poem #1." In *Voices of the
Rainbow: Contemporary Poetry by American
Indians*. Kenneth Rosen, ed. New York:
Seaver Books, 1975, 17.
"Deer Dance/For Your Return." *Columbia*, 1
(Autumn 1977), 9. Reprinted in *The Indian
Rio Grande: Recent Poems From Three
Cultures*. Gene Frumkin and Stanley Noyes,
eds. Los Cerillos, New Mexico: San Marcos
Press, 1977, 9-11, and in Silko,
Storyteller, 188-190.
"Deer Song." *The Journal of Ethnic Studies*,
2:2 (Summer 1974), 69. Reprinted in Rosen,
Voices of the Rainbow, 13, and in Silko,
Storyteller, 200-202.
"Four Mountain Wolves." In *Laguna Woman*.
Leslie Marmon Silko. Greenfield Center, New
York: Greenfield Review Press, 1974, 19-20.
Reprinted in Rosen, *Voices of the Rainbow*,
19.
"Hawk and Snake" (Chinle, June 1972). *Chicago
Review*, 24:4 (Spring 1973), 8. Reprinted in
Silko, *Laguna Woman*, 30, and in Rosen,
Voices of the Rainbow, 28.
"Horses at Valley Store." *Chicago Review*, 24:4
(Spring 1973), 99. Reprinted in Silko,
Laguna Woman, 32; in Rosen, *Voices of the
Rainbow*, 29; in *The Next World: Poems by 32
Third World Americans*. Joseph Bruchac, ed.
Trumansburg, New York: The Crossing Press,
1978, 175; in *The Remembered Earth: An
Anthology of Contemporary Native American
Literature*. Geary Hobson, ed. Albuquerque,
New Mexico: Red Earth Press, 1979, 208; and
in Silko, *Storyteller*, 181.
"How to Write a Poem About the Sky." In White,
The First Skin Around Me, 76. Reprinted in
Silko, *Storyteller*, 177.
"Incantation." In Frumkin, *The Indian Rio
Grande*, 101-102.

"In Cold Storm Light." *Quetzal*, 2:3 (Summer
1972), 46. Reprinted in *Chicago Review*,
24:4 (Spring 1973), 96; in Silko, *Laguna
Woman*, 28; in Rosen, *Voices of the Rainbow*,
26; and in Silko, *Storyteller*, 178.
"Indian Song: Survival." *Chicago Review*, 24:4
(Spring 1973), 96. Reprinted in Silko,
Laguna Woman, 25-27; in *Carriers of the
Dream Wheel: Contemporary Native American
Poetry*. Duane Niatum, ed. New York: Harper
and Row, Publishers, 1975, 229; in Rosen,
Voices of the Rainbow, 23, in *Come to
Power: Eleven Contemporary American Indian
Poets*. Dick Lourie, ed. Trumansburg, New
York: The Crossing Press, 1974, 95; and in
Silko, *Storyteller*, 35-37.
"Laughing and Laughing." In Lourie, *Come to
Power*, 99.
"Love Poem." In Silko, *Laguna Woman*, 16.
Reprinted in Lourie, *Come to Power*, 100,
and in Rosen, *Voices of the Rainbow*, 11.
"Mesita Men." In Silko, *Laguna Woman*, 22.
"Poem for Ben Barney." In Silko, *Laguna Woman*,
14-15. Reprinted in Niatum, *Carriers of the
Dream Wheel*, 228, and in Rosen, *Voices of
the Rainbow*, 18.
"Poem for Myself and Mei: Concerning
Abortion." *Journal of Ethnic Studies*, 2:2
(Summer 1974), 66. Reprinted in Silko,
Laguna Woman, 6-7; in Rosen, *Voices of the
Rainbow*, 12; and in Silko, *Storyteller*,
122-123.
"Prayer to the Pacific." *Chicago Review*, 24:4
(Spring 1973), 93. Reprinted in Silko,
Laguna Woman, 23-24; in Lourie, *Come to
Power*, 98; in Niatum, *Carriers of the Dream
Wheel*, 226-227; in Rosen, *Voices of the
Rainbow*, 22; in *Southwest: A Contemporary
Anthology*. Karl and Jane Kopp, eds.
Albuquerque, New Mexico: Red Earth Press,
1977, 389-390; and in Silko, *Storyteller*,
179.

"Preparations." *Chicago Review,* 24:4 (Spring
    1973), 100. Reprinted in Silko, *Laguna
    Woman,* 33; in Rosen, *Voices of the Rainbow,*
    30; in Bruchac, *The Next World,* 176; and in
    Silko, *Storyteller,* 203.
"Prophecy of Old Woman Mountain." *The Journal
    of Ethnic Studies,* 2:2 (Summer 1974), 70.
"Si' Anh Aash." In Silko, *Laguna Woman,* 21.
"Skeleton Fixer's Story." *Sun Tracks: An
    American Indian Literary Magazine,* 4
    (1978), 2-3. Reprinted in Silko,
    Storyteller, 242-245.
"Slim Man Canyon." In Silko, *Laguna Woman,* 17.
    Reprinted in Lourie, *Come to Power*; in
    Rosen, *Voices of the Rainbow,* 21; in Kopp
    and Kopp, *Southwest,* 331; and in Hobson,
    The Remembered Earth, 208.
"Snow Elk." *Quetzal,* 2, Summer 1972, 46.
"Story from Bear Country." *A: A Journal of
    Contemporary Literature* 2:2 (Fall 1977), 4-
    6. Reprinted in *Antaeus,* 27 (Autumn 1977),
    62; in Hobson, *The Remembered Earth,* 209;
    in Silko, *Storyteller,* 204-207; and in
    *Songs From This Earth On Turtle's Back:
    Contemporary American Indian Poetry.* Joseph
    Bruchac, ed. Greenfield Center, New York:
    Greenfield Review Press, 1983, 225-227.
"Storytelling." *The Journal of Ethnic Studies,*
    2:2 (Summer 1974), 72-74. Reprinted in
    Silko, *Storyteller,* 94-98.
"Sun Children." *Quetzal,* 2:3 (Summer 1972),
    47. Reprinted in *Chicago Review,* 24:4
    (Spring 1973), 97; in Silko, *Laguna Woman,*
    29; and in Rosen, *Voices of the Rainbow,*
    26.
"The Time We Climbed Snake Mountain." *Chicago
    Review* 24:4 (Spring 1973), 99. Reprinted in
    Silko, *Laguna Woman,* 31; in Lourie, *Come to
    Power,* 97; in Rosen, *Voices of the Rainbow,*
    29; and in Silko, *Storyteller,* 76-77.
"Toe'osh: A Laguna Coyote Story." In Silko,
    Laguna Woman, 9-11. Reprinted in Niatum,
    Carriers of the Dream Wheel, 223-225; in

Rosen, *Voices of the Rainbow*, 14-17; in
Bruchac, *The Next World*, 176-178; in *The
Third Woman: Minority Woman Writers of the
United States*. Dexter Fisher, ed. Boston:
Houghton Mifflin Co., 1980, 93-95; in
Silko, *Storyteller*, 236-239; and in
Bruchac, *Songs From This Earth on Turtle's
Back*, 228-229.
"When Sun Came to Riverwoman." *Greenfield
Review*, 3:2 (1973), 67. Reprinted in Silko,
Laguna Woman, 12-13; in Rosen, *Voices of
the Rainbow*, 9; in Bruchac, *The Next World*,
174-175; and in Hobson, *The Remembered
Earth*, 207.
"Where Mountain Lion Laid Down With Deer."
February 1973. *Northwest Review*, 13:2
(1973), 34. Reprinted in Silko, *Laguna
Woman*, 18; in rosen, *Voices of the Rainbow*,
8; in *I Am The Fire of Time: The Voices of
Native American Women*. Jane B. Katz, ed.
New York: E.P. Dutton, 1977, 165; in
Fisher, *The Third Woman*, 92-93; in Silko,
Storyteller, 199-200, and in Bruchac, *Songs
From This Earth on Turtle's Back*, 224.

Short Fiction

"A Geronimo Story." In Lourie, *Come to Power*,
81-94. Reprinted in Rosen, *The Man to send
Rain Clouds*, 128-144, and in Silko,
Storyteller, 212-223.
"Bravura." In Rosen, *The man to Send Rain
Clouds*, 149-154.
"Coyote Holds a Full House in His Hand." *Tri-
Quarterly*, 48 (Spring 1980), 166-174.
Reprinted in Silko, *Storyteller*, 257-265.
"From a Novel Not Yet Titled." *The Journal of
Ethnic Studies*, 3:1 (Spring 1975), 72-87.
"Gallup, New Mexico - Indian Capital of the
World." *New America: A Review*, 2:3 (Summer-
Fall 1976), 30-32.
"Humaweepi, the Warrior Priest" (excerpt from
a novel). In Rosen, *The Man to Send Rain
Clouds*, 161-168.

"Lullaby." *Chicago Review*, 26:1 (Summer 1974),
10-17. Reprinted, *Yardbird Reader*, 3
(1974), 87-95, and in Kopp and Kopp,
Southwest, 242-249.
"Storyteller." *Puerto del Sol*, 14:1 (Fall
1975), 11-25. Reprinted in Hobson, *The
Remembered Earth*, 195-206; in Fisher, *The
Third Woman*, 70-83; and in Silko,
Storyteller, 17-32.
"The Man to Send Rain Clouds." *New Mexico
Quarterly*, 38:4 (Winter/Spring 1969), 133-
136. Reprinted in Rosen, *The Man to Send
Rain Clouds*, 3-8; in Katz, *I Am the Fire of
Time*, 156-161; and in Silko, *Storyteller*,
183-186.
"Tony's Story." *Thunderbird*, (literary
magazine of the students of the University
of New Mexico) (1969), 2-4. Reprinted in
Redbook, 44:3 (January 1975), 75-76: 46-48;
in Rosen, *The Man to Send Rain Clouds*, 69-
78; and in Silko, *Storyteller*, 123-129.
"Uncle Tony's Goat." In Rosen, *The Man to Send
Rain Clouds*, 93-100. Reprinted in Silko,
Storyteller, 171-178.
"Yellow Woman." In Rosen, *The Man to Send Rain
Clouds*, 33-45. Reprinted in Silko,
Storyteller, 54-62.

Articles and Essays

"An Old-Time Indian Attack Conducted in Two
Parts." *Yardbird Reader*, 5 (1976), 77-84.
Reprinted, *Shantih*, 4:2 (Summer/Fall 1979),
3-4, and in Hobson, *The Remembered Earth*,
211-215.
"Foreword," to *Border Towns of the Navajo
Nation*. Aaron Yava. Alamo, California:
Holmganger Press, 1975, 3-4. Originally in
Yardbird Reader, 3 (1974), 98-103.
"Language and Literature from a Pueblo Indian
Perspective." In *Opening Up the Canyon:
Selected Papers from the English Institute*.
Leslie Fiedler and Houston A. Baker, Jr.

eds. Baltimore: John Hopkins Univ. Press,
1981, 54-72.

Plays

"Lullaby." San Francisco City Arts Commission
performance, 1976.

Film Scripts

"Coronado Expedition of 1540." Script sent to
Marlon Brando. Was adapted by Harry Brown
in 1977 but was not used.
"Estoyehmuut and the Kunideeyah" (Arrowboy and
the Destroyers). Laguna Pueblo Narrative
Adapted for Film by Leslie Marmon Silko and
Dennis W. Carr. National Endowment for the
Humanities, Media Division, 1981.

Interviews and Autobiographical Information

"A Conversation with Leslie Silko." Videotape
1975. Lawrence J. Evers and Dennis W. Carr.
Available for viewing at Southwest Folklore
Center Archive, University of Arizona.
"A Conversation with Leslie Marmon Silko." *Sun
Tracks: An American Indian Literary
Magazine*, 3:1 (Fall 1976), 28-33.
Autobiographical Information. Silko, *Laguna
Woman*, 34-35.
Autobiographical Information. Letter to
Abraham Chapman, in Chapman, *Literature of
the American Indians: Views and
Interpretations*. New York: New American
Library, 1975, 5-6.
"Leslie Silko: Storyteller." Interview.
Persona, James Fitzgerald and John Hudak,
eds. 1980, 21-38.
"The Novel and Oral Tradition: An Interview
with Leslie Marmon Silko." Elaine Jahner.
Book Review Forum, 5:3 (1981), 383-388.
"Stories and Their Tellers: A Conversation
with Leslie Marmon Silko." In Fisher, *The
Third Woman*, 18-23.

III. Selected Secondary Sources

Criticism of *Ceremony*

Allen, Paula Gunn. "A Stranger in My Own
Life: Alienation in American Indian Prose
and Poetry." *MELUS*, 7 (Summer 1980), 3-19.
Allen suggests that a preoccupation with the
process of alienation is central to contemporary
American Indian writing. In a discussion of such
writers as Silko, N. Scott Momaday, and James
Welch, Allen finds that alienation is characteristic of the life of the Indian "half or mixed
blood." She asserts that Tayo is an outsider
before his experience of war. He is mocked by
the Lagunas because of his green eyes. He is not
accepted by the tribe because the tribe does not
approve of mixed blood. Silko offers a positive
note within the novel, Allen argues. Tayo is
finally able to gain acceptance of self through
the ceremonial rite.

Allen, Paula Gunn. "The Psychological
Landscape of *Ceremony*." *American Indian
Quarterly* 5, (1979), 7-12.
The critic argues that to Native Americans "the
land and the People are the same. The earth is
the source and the being of the People. Thus,
Tayo's illness is a result of separation from the
ancient unity of person with land, and his healing is a result of his recognition of this one-
ness." Allen traces Tayo's illness, and the
ceremony which leads to his healing. Although
she relates this process in Jungian terms, Allen
explains that a Jungian interpretation misses the
essential point that Tayo's psychological illness
is also the illness of the world, and the land
itself. The author argues that Tayo finally
comes to understand "that the true nature of
being is magical, and that the proper duty of the
creatures and of men is to live in harmony with
what is."

Allen, Paula Gunn. "The Feminine Landscape of
Leslie Silko's *Ceremony.*" *Studies in
American Indian Literature: Critical Essays
and Course Designs.* Paula Gunn Allen, ed.
New York: Modern Language Association of
America, 1983, 127-133.
The critic argues that there are two types of
male and female characters in *Ceremony*: those who
belong to the earth spirit and live in harmony
with her, and those who live to destroy the earth
spirit. Allen suggests that *Ceremony* is the tale
of a character who is healed and joins the first
category of characters. The critic traces the
connections among the land, womanness, and the
earth spirit and suggests that Tayo experiences
an "initiation into womanhood" during the course
of the novel which results in his movement from
isolated warrior to spiritually integrated
person.

Beidler, Peter G., and Ruoff, Lavonne A. "A
Discussion of *Winter in the Blood.*"
American Indian Quarterly, 4 (1978), 159-
68.
This article is an edited transcript of a
discussion which followed the presentation of six
papers on *Winter in the Blood*, delivered in
Chicago in 1977 at the national conference of the
Modern Language Association. Although the
article deals chiefly with Welch's novel, there
is also some analysis of Silko's work, *Ceremony*.
One participant notes that both works revolve
around pairs of brothers, each pair made up of
one living and one dead sibling. It is also
argued during the discussion, that Silko's novel
is a very literary work which makes use of both
Western and Indian traditions.

Beidler, Peter G. "Animals and Human
Development in the Contemporary American
Indian Novel." *Western American Literature*,
14 (Summer 1979), 133-148.

Beidler argues that *House Made of Dawn* (1966), by
N. Scott Momaday; *Winter in the Blood* (1974), by
James Welch; and *Ceremony* (1970, by Silko, all
tell the same story. In each work an alienated
Indian hero drifts about until, recognizing meaningful analogies between himself and the animals
around him, he puts himself in touch with their
lives and finds his proper place in the modern
world. In Silko's work it is important to note,
the critic states, that Ts'its'tsi, nako, the
creator of everything in Silko's world, and the
creator of her story, is an animal. Tayo loses
his respect for animals, the critic argues, while
he is in the company of white men, but during the
course of the novel he regains his concern for
them. Finally, Beidler points out, by imitating
the Mexican cattle Tayo makes himself and the
land "safe again--for a time--from the
destroyers."

    Beidler, Peter G. "Animals and Theme in
       Ceremony." *American Indian Quarterly*, 5
       (1979), 13-18.
Beidler argues that although *Ceremony* is a work
about people, "it is impossible to understand the
people, their problems, or the solutions to those
problems without becoming aware of the role which
animals play in the novel." The critic argues
that Tayo's illness stems from his identification
with the white man's attitude toward animal life.
Beidler traces this attitude as it is developed
in the novel, and explains how Tayo's ceremony
hinges on regaining respect for animal life
through identification with animals, chiefly the
Mexican cattle. Tayo learns from the animals,
Beidler argues, what to resist and what to
accept.

    Bell, Robert C. "Circular Design in
       Ceremony." *American Indian Quarterly*, 5
       (1979), 47-62.
Bell argues that in *Ceremony* the hoop ritual
"recapitulates, in astonishing detail, the pro-

cedures set forth in the Coyote Transformation
rite, in the Myth of Red Antway, Male Evilway.
The critic provides a comparison of the two
texts, and suggests that the rite is a likely
source for the hoop ceremony at the middle of
Silko's work (138-153).

> Buller, Galen. "New Interpretations of Native
> American Literature: A Survival
> Technique." *American Indian Culture and
> Research Journal*, 4:1-2 (1980), 165-77.

Buller argues that "American Indian literature is
something unique, and, as such, should be taught
as something distinctive from American literature
written by non-Indian authors." Several attributes of the literature, Buller points out, are
"a reverence for words, a sense of place, a
feeling for and participation in ritual, and an
affirmation that there exists uniquely Indian
assumptions about the nature of the universe."
The critic points out how *Ceremony* contains these
attributes.

> Evers, Larry. "A Response: Going Along With
> the Story." *American Indian Quarterly*, 5
> (1979), 71-75.

Evers argues that stories, such as *Ceremony*, "at
once teach survival and demonstrate it." He explains how *Ceremony* gives its characters control
of their world. Evers goes on to discuss the
criticism of American Indian literature.

> Hoilman, Dennis R. "A World Made of
> Stories: An Interpretation of Leslie
> Silko's *Ceremony*." *South Dakota Review*, 17
> (1979-80), 54-66.

Hoilman argues that *Ceremony* is an attempt "to
inform the non-Indian reader about Keresan culture and to enable him to participate a little in
Keresan thought patterns." The critic explains
that *Ceremony* is a difficult book for non-Indians
to understand because of its structure and
because of Laguna mythology. Hoilman traces the

novel's structure and points out how the myths
surface and resurface in the work. Hoilman also
comments on the function of the myths within
Ceremony.

Hunter, Carol. "American Indian
    Literature." *MELUS*, 8:2 (Summer 1981), 82-
    85.
Hunter discusses American Indian literature in
the 1980's and makes predictions about the
literature's future. The critic explains that
American Indian literature is a multi-ethnic
literature. Dividing the literature into two
categories, traditional oral literature and
modern fiction, the author deals with each branch
and explains the connection which one often finds
between the latter and the former. In this context, the critic explains how Silko incorporated
oral literature into her novel. Hunter argues
that Silko relied upon "Keresan ceremonial tales,
focusing on mythical events and characters to
tell the story of a battle-fatigued war veteran
who must go through the traditional Pueblo healing ceremony to be cured."

Jahner, Elaine. "An Act of Attention: Event
    Structure in *Ceremony*." *American Indian
    Quarterly*, 5 (1979), 37-46.
Jahner argues that *Ceremony* has an "energy" that
engages readers. She explains that one way to
explain this energy is to point out that it stems
from the experience of event rather than sequen-
tially motivated action. The critic explains
Silko's use of event structure and suggests that
"progress made toward understanding event may be
progress toward understanding relationships
between oral and written literature."

Larson, Charles R. *American Indian Fiction*.
    Albuquerque: University of New Mexico
    Press, 1978, 150-161.
Larson follows through the novel's action and
provides a running analysis. Among the elements

he brings to light are: the novel's recurring
images; the way group-felt experiences are a
concern of the work; the major themes of the
novel, as he sees them; the significance of the
Mexican cattle; and the way that poems function
within *Ceremony*. Larson states that Silko has
reached beyond her contemporaries "because of her
faith in the redeeming value of language and
ritual." He views the novel's final image of
dawn as a sign of hope.

Lincoln, Kenneth. *Native American Renaissance*.
     Berkeley, CA: University of California
     Press, 1983, 233-251.
After examining the nature of Indian storytelling, and Silko's "Storyteller," the critic devotes several pages to a discussion of *Ceremony*.
Lincoln begins with background on Laguna ethnology and the Marmon family. The critic defines
the structure of Silko's novel and states, "In
Ceremony, Silko enters a half-breed's fractured
consciousness to bridge Western transitions
between male and female, adult and child, history
and myth, dark and light, Indian and White."
Tracing the influence of thought-woman, Lincoln
views the novel as a word ceremony in which "the
narrator is the story." The critic explains the
significance of the color "blue" in the novel,
and traces the movement of the novel from sunrise
to sunrise, from spring through a complete
seasonal cycle.

McFarland, Ronald E. "Leslie Silko's Story of
     Stories." *A: a journal of contemporary
     literature*. 4:2 (Fall 1979), 18-23.
As well as presenting information about traditional Pueblo storytelling, the critic analyzes
the narrative strategy of *Ceremony*. McFarland
contends: "There are three major narrative
strands in this novel: 1. the Pueblo tale of
curing and pacification; 2. the intentionally
clichéed story of the Indian in post-World War II
United States; 3. Tayo's story." The critic

also examines the fluid nature of time within the
work, and comments upon *Ceremony's* lack of
chapter divisions.

Mitchell, Carol. "*Ceremony* as Ritual."
    American Indian Quarterly, 5 (1979), 27-35.
Mitchell explains that *Ceremony* can be viewed as
three simultaneous planes which interweave
throughout the work: the human plane, the
socio/cultural plane, and the myth/ritual
plane. The critic argues that "the reader's
understanding of the traditional materials found
in the myth/ritual plane is crucial to the understanding of the whole novel." Mitchell explores
the traditional myths, curing stories, and chants
and explains their relationship to the novel.

Ortiz, Simon J. "Towards a National Indian
    Literature: Cultural Authenticity in
    Nationalism." *MELUS*, 8:2 (Summer 1981), 7-
    12.
The critic explains that it is the primary
element of a national impulse that makes native
Americans use foreign ritual, ideas, and material
in their own Indian terms. On the issue of the
use of non-native languages, the author main-
tains, "it is entirely possible for a people to
retain and maintain their lives through the use
of any language." Ortiz argues that this mainten-
ance, or resistance, has in the past been carried
on through the use of the oral tradition, but is
now being continued in contemporary Indian
literature. *Ceremony*, the critic asserts, is an
example of this Indian resistance. Ortiz states
that the forces of colonialism are described as
"witchery" in Silko's novel. Tayo's triumph over
these forces, through his use of storytelling, is
representative, the critic feels, of the way oral
tradition and Indian literature can create a
national Indian literature.

Sands, Kathleen M. and Ruoff, A. LaVonne. "A
    Discussion of *Ceremony*." *American Indian
    Quarterly*, 5 (1979), 63-70.

The article is an edited transcript of the
discussion which followed the oral summaries of
six papers on *Ceremony* delivered at the 1978
annual meeting of the Rocky Mountain Modern
Language Association. Among the topics covered
are how the novel is simultaneously a process of
literature and a curative process in and of
itself, how the novel contains elements that are
distinctively American Indian in nature, and how
the work makes use of "fragmentation."

    Sands, Kathleen M. "Preface: A Symposium
        Issue." *American Indian Quarterly*, 5
        (1979), 1-5.
The critic states that *Ceremony* is worthy of
study because the novel "affirms the reality of a
truly Indian fiction and is obviously an important work in the mainstream of American letters."
Sands felt that *Ceremony* would make an excellent
subject for the American Indian literature seminar at the 1978 Rocky Mountain Modern Language
Association meeting. She sent out a call for
papers, and the six papers chosen for the seminar
are the content for the special *American Indian
Quarterly* issue which this article prefaces. The
author notes that the papers fall into general
categories: the first two papers focus on the
relationship of the protagonist to nature and the
land, the second pair of papers focus on the way
in which ritual provides a means of curing for
Tayo, and the structuring of event and renewal of
myth in the novel leads to the focus of the last
two papers. Sands provides her readers with a
brief summary of the novel and also a summary of
the history of the Laguna Pueblo, illustrating
its relationship to the themes and background of
the novel.

    Scarberry, Susan J. "Memory as Medicine: The
        Power of Recollection in *Ceremony*."
        American Indian Quarterly, 5 (19779), 19-
        26.

The critic traces the way that memory functions
as an element of the novel. Scarberry points out
that as the novel unfolds, Tayo is at the mercy
of his memories which manipulate him and almost
force him to commit suicide. Gradually, however,
his memories become more and more positive, the
manipulation ceases, and the curative process
begins. Scarberry states, "the novel then
becomes a working out of Tayo's control of his
memory and of his corresponding growth into
wholeness. . . ."

   Seyersted, Per. "Leslie Marmon Silko."
   Western Writers Series, 45, 25-36.
Seyersted views *Ceremony* as a book which deals
with the "dark aspects of modern Indian life,
especially in the younger reservation people who
are most exposed to outside influences." The
critic argues that veterans, such as Tayo, are
especially bitter toward whites because they have
been given equal status in the military, only to
return to their position as second-class citizens
when they return home. Seyersted states that
Tayo is furthermore in despair because he cannot
accept himself. The critic traces the steps of
the ceremony which allows Tayo to become cured.
The author gives an explanation of Silko's use of
Pueblo myth, and also comments on the position of
the medicine man in Navaho society. Seyersted
argues that Silko's addition of romance to the
Indian experience composed of myth, history, and
realism is a remarkable achievement. Seyersted's
work also contains a great deal of background on
Silko, and an excellent bibliography.

   Velie, Alan R. "Leslie Silko's *Ceremony*: A
   Laguna Grail Story." *Four American Indian
   Literary Masters*. Norman: University of
   Oklahoma Press, 1982, 105-121.
Velie argues that Silko's work belongs to a tra-
dition and form older than the novel--the grail
romance. Although the critic states that Silko
was not familiar with the grail legend at the

time she wrote *Ceremony*, he contends that both
the grail romances and the novel are based on the
fundamental idea that a man's health and behavior
have grave consequences for his land. Velie
points out numerous parallels between *Ceremony*
and the grail romances.

Velie, Alan R. "*Winter in the Blood* as Comic
Novel." *American Indian Quarterly*, 4
(1978), 141-47.
Although this article deals chiefly with Welch's
novel, the critic also discusses *Ceremony*. Velie
argues that *Ceremony* is a comic novel which ends
on a positive note.

Wilson, Norma. "Outlook for Survival."
Denver Quarterly, 14:4 (Winter 1980), 22-
30.
Wilson traces Silko's use of the oral tradition
in *Ceremony*. The critic points out that it is
the process of renewal found in the oral tradition which allows for the important potential of
the form. Wilson points out that by using the
English language, Silko is able to convey "what
would have earlier been carried on the tongue.
In this way, the ceremony can reach more people.
It may have a greater potential for healing."

Reviews of *Ceremony*

American Indian Culture and Research Journal.
vol. 4, no. 4, 1980, 140-147.
American West. Volume 16, May/June 1979, 48.
ASAIL Newsletter. Volume 2, Number 1, (Spring
1978), 8-12.
Best Sellers. XXXVII, August 1977, 138-139.
Book List. LXXIII, April 1, 1977, 1147.
Book World. (Washington Post) April 24, 1977,
E4.
Choice. LIV, July 1977, 684.
Christian Science Monitor. August 24, 1977,
31. ILL 10/19
Harper's. CCLIV, June 1977, 80.

Kliatt Paperback Guide. XII, (Fall 1978), 14.
L.A. Times Book Review. August 28, 1977, 26.
Library Journal. Volume 102, January 15,
     1977, 220.
New Leader. LX, June 6, 1977, 14.
New York Review of Books. Volume 24, May 1977,
     39.
New York Times Book Review. June 12, 1977, 15.
New York Times Book Review. April 23, 1978,
     43.
Newsweek. Volume 90, July 4, 1977, 73.
Prairie Schooner. Volume 51, (Winter 1977-78),
     415-416.
Publishers' Weekly. CCXI, January 24, 1977,
     329.
Publishers' Weekly. CCXIII, February 27, 1978,
     153.
The Great Lakes Review, vol. 6, no. 1, Summer
     1979, 115-116.
Thoreau Quarterly Journal, vol. 10, no. 3,
     1978, 37.
Western American Literature. vol. 12, no. 3,
     1977, 242-243.

Biographical Sources

A Directory of American Fiction Writers. New
     York: Poets and Writers, Inc., 1976.
A Directory of American Poets. New York: Poets
     and Writers, Inc., 1975.
New York Times. May 19, 1981.
New York Times. May 25, 1981.
New York Times. March 27, 1983.
New York Times Magazine. December 27, 1981.
*The Next World: Poems by Third World
     Americans,* ed. by Joseph Bruchac.
     Trumansburg, New York: The Crossing Press,
     1978.
This Song Remembers. Boston: Houghton Mifflin,
     1980.
Time. June 1, 1981.
Time. August 8, 1983.

*Voices of the Rainbow: Contemporary Poetry by
American Indians,* ed. by Kenneth Rosen. New
York: Seaver, 1975.

Virginia Driving Hawk Sneve
(1933 -)

I. Biography

Of Brule Sioux ancestry, Sneve was born in
Rosebud, South Dakota. She holds B.S. and M.Ed.
degrees from South Dakota State University.
Sneve taught and was a guidance counselor in
South Dakota before becoming an editor for Brevet
Press of Sioux Falls. Sneve is a member of the
Rosebud Sioux Tribe and has served as a member of
the board of directors for the United Sioux
Tribes Cultural Arts Council. She is also a
member of the National League of American Pen
Women and of South Dakota Press Women. In 1971
Jimmy Yellow Hawk, one of a series of juvenile
novels which Sneve has written, was named the
best work of the year in the American Indian
category by the Interracial Council for Minority
Books for Children. Sneve resides in Flandreau,
South Dakota.

II. Primary Sources

Novels

High Elk's Treasure. New York: Holiday
House, 1972.
The novel begins with the story of High Elk, a
Brule Sioux who settles on the Dakota Reservation
in 1876 and begins a herd of horses from an old,
lame mare. High Elk's herd eventually becomes
big and famous until hard times cause the dimin-
ishment of the herd to the point that by the time
of Joe High Elk, High Elk's greatgrandson, only
one filly remains. Joe and his father, William,
hope to begin the famous herd anew from the
filly, and when Joe finds High Elk's treasure, an
old leather pouch containing a drawing of Rain-
in-the-Face killing Custer and High Elk leading
his mare away from the battle, the dream appears
possible.

Jimmy Yellow Hawk. New York: Holiday House,
   1972.
Little Jim Yellow Hawk is ten years old and wants
to change his name from Little Jim because his
friends make fun of him. After his grandfather
tells him a story of a boy who saved his tribe by
trapping, Little Jim decides to change his name
by becoming a famous trapper--since, according to
Sioux custom, a boy can earn his adult name
through deeds. Little Jim begins trapping and
traps a mink, an act which wins the admiration of
everyone and which causes Little Jim to be called
Jimmy Yellow Hawk, much to his satisfaction.

When Thunders Spoke. New York: Holiday
   House, 1974.
Fifteen-year-old Norman Two Bull is the third
generation of his family to live on the Dakota
reservation. In the beginning of the novel,
Norman trades agates from the nearby Butte of
Thunders for candy at the local trading post, as
he has been doing for some time. After his
grandfather has a dream and tells Norman to climb
the butte, Norman goes to the butte and finds an
old coup stick while searching for the agates.
The coup stick is wakan and greatly changes the
fortunes of the family. Norman now sells his
agates to the trading post owner, and Norman's
father becomes foreman of the tribal ranch. In
the end, Norman resists materialism and refuses
to sell agates from the butte, and he resists
offers to buy the coup stick. After being
brought home by Norman, the coup stick has magi-
cally become bright and fresh, but in the novel's
conclusion Norman, along with his father and
grandfather, return the stick to the Butte of
Thunders where it was found.

Betrayed. New York: Holiday House, 1974.
Based on an historical event which took place in
1862, this novel deals with the revolt of the
Santee Sioux against white settlers in the
Minnesota Valley at the time of the U.S. Civil

War. White Lodge's band of Santee take several
women and children as hostages. Charger, a young
Teton Sioux, learns of the hostages, and after a
vision which tells him he must rescue the hostages Charger goes with other Teton braves and
barters for the release of the whites. The Teton
braves then free the whites. The novel ends with
a grim execution of the Santee responsible for
the slaughter of whites during the uprising.

> *The Chichi Hoohoo Bogeyman.* New York:
> Holiday House, 1975.

Three young girls, MaryJo and her two American
Indian cousins, have listened to stories of evil
spirits. When the girls are menaced by an evil-
looking man, they escape by canoe on the Sioux
River and make up the name "chichi hoohoo bogey-
man" for the mysterious figure to combine the
names for dangerous spirits of the Sioux, Hopi,
and white.

Other Booklength Works

> (Editor) *South Dakota Geographic Names.* Sioux
>   Falls, S.D.: Brevet Press, 1973.
> *The Dakota's Heritage.* Sioux Falls, S.D.:
>   Brevet Press, 1973.
> *They Led a Nation.* Sioux Falls, S.D.: Brevet
>   Press, 1975.
> *Three Dakota Grandmother Stories: Health
>   Lessons for Young Readers.* New York:
>   Association on American Indian Affairs,
>   1975.
> *The Twelve Moons.* New York: Houghton Mifflin,
>   1977. This is a 32 page children's book.

III. Selected Secondary Sources

Reviews

High Elk's Treasure
  Center for Children's Books Bulletin. Volume
    26, February 1973, 97.
  Choice. Volume 14, November 1977, 1178.
  Kirkus Review. Volume 40, September 15, 1972,
    1100.
  Library Journal. Volume 98, March 15, 1973,
    1008.
  New York Times Book Review. Pt. 2, November 5,
    1972, 14.
  Social Education. Volume 37, December 1973,
    789.

Jimmy Yellow Hawk
  Booklist. Volume 69, October 15, 1972, 178.
  Center for Children's Books Bulletin. Volume
    26, February 1973, 98.
  Choice. Volume 14, November 1977, 1178.
  Commonweal. Volume 97, February 23, 1973, 473.
  Horn Book Magazine. Volume 48, August 1972,
    383.
  Kirkus Review. Volume 40, March 15, 1972, 325.
  Library Journal. Volume 97, June 15, 1972,
    2240.
  New York Times Book Review. Pt. 2, November 5,
    1972, 14.

When Thunders Spoke
  Center for Children's Books Bulletin. Volume
    28, November 1974, 53.
  Elementary English. Volume 52, April 1975,
    485.
  Kirkus Review. Volume 42, May 1, 1974, 481.
  Library Journal. Volume 99, September 15,
    1974, 2298.
  Publishers Weekly. Volume 205, May 27, 1974,
    65.
  Social Education. Volume 39, March 1975, 174.

Betrayed
> *American Libraries.* Volume 6, March 1975, 166.
> *Booklist.* Volume 71, November 15, 1974, 345.
> *Best Sellers.* Volume 34, February 15, 1975,
>   519.
> *Center for Children's Books Bulletin.* Volume
>   28, April 1975, 139.
> *Kirkus Review.* Volume 42, November 15, 1974,
>   1203.
> *New York Times Book Review.* January 19, 1975,
>   8.
> *Publishers Weekly.* Volume 206, October 7,
>   1974, 62.
> *School Library Journal.* Volume 21, January
>   1975, 57.

Biographical Sources

> *Children's Literature in Review.* vol. 2. ed.
>   by Carolyn Riley. Detroit: Gale Research
>   Co., 1976.
> *Contemporary Authors.* vol. 49. Detroit: Gale
>   Research Co., 1975.
> *Horn Book.* August 1972.
> *Sioux Falls Argus-Leader.* August 5, 1973.
> *Something About the Author,* ed. by Anne
>   Commire. Detroit: Gale Research Co., 1976.

Hyemeyohsts Storm
(1935 -)

I. Biography

Hyemeyohsts Storm, a Northern Cheyenne, was born
in Lame Deer, Montana. He studied briefly at
several colleges, including Oakland City College
in California and Eastern Montana College.
Storm's first novel, *Seven Arrows* (1972), was the
first novel published as part of Harper & Row's
Native American Publishing Program and generated
a great deal of commentary, both positive and
negative, when it appeared. Storm has since
published a second novel, *Song of Heyoehkah*.
Storm currently lives in Nevada City, California
and is working on a third novel, *Lightningbolt*.
"*Seven Arrows* was my South book," he states.
"The *Song of Heyoehkah* was my West book.
Lightningbolt is my North book." A collection of
Storm's short stories, as yet untitled, will soon
be published by Fink Verlag in Munich, Germany.

II. Primary Sources

Novels

Seven Arrows. New York: Harper & Row, 1972.
Storm blends oral tradition of the plains Indians
with photography, graphics, history, and fiction
to create a panorama of the plains Indian experience from the first encounters with the white
man to the near present. The novel tells of the
destruction of individuals and of the People, and
it documents the desecration of Indian culture
through confrontation and intermixture with the
whites.

The Song of Heyoekhah. New York: Harper &
Row, 1979.
Storm's second novel blends history, fantasy, and
fiction with American Indian cosmology and oral

tradition to create a work which becomes a vision
quest for the reader. Alternating threads of the
narrative tell of the vision quest of a young
Indian woman named Estchimah, of a small group of
Indians who have survived massacre by whites and
other Indians, and of three young white gold
hunters who wander into the world of the plains
Indians. In a fascinating reversal, Storm
details the experiences of Calvin, one of the
whites who becomes Dancing Tree, one of the
People.

Selected Shorter Publications

Short Fiction

"From *Seven Arrows*." In *Literature of the
American Indians: Views and Interpreta-
tions*. Abraham Chapman, ed. New York: The
New American Library, 1975, 137-148.

III. Selected Secondary Sources

Criticism of *Seven Arrows*

Brumble, H. David III. "Anthropologists,
Novelists and Indian Sacred Material." *The
Canadian Review of American Studies*, 11:1
(Spring 1980), 31-48.
Brumble explores the awkward position writers--
Indian or white--find themselves in when attempting to deal with Indian sacred material. The
author traces changing attitudes toward the
explication of Indian sacred materials in this
century and compares Storm's *Seven Arrows* to
Frank Water's *Book of the Hopi*. Each book is,
according to Brumble, "a deeply felt, non-
professional account of Indian materials colored
and reshaped by the moral-aesthetic concerns of
an Anglo-educated individual intelligence."
Brumble cites criticism condemning inaccuracies
in *Seven Arrows*.

Costo, Rupert. "*Seven Arrows* Desecrates
     Cheyenne." *The Indian Historian*, 5:2
     (Summer 1972), 41-42.
Although technically a review, Costo's brief
essay is significant because it presents an
Indian perspective of Storm's novel. Costo lists
a number of facts and details in *Seven Arrows*
which are incorrect or distort Cheyenne tradition
and religion and states, "The book is a White
Man's interpretation of the Cheyenne."

Larson, Charles R. "*Seven Arrows*: Saga of the
     American Indian." *Books Abroad* 47 (1973),
     88-92.
In this early essay, Larson mistakenly declares
Seven Arrows to be "the first novel by an
American Indian," and adds that it is "the most
extraordinary book I have ever read." Considering what he calls the book's unique "topography,"
Larson finds *Seven Arrows* to be a "perfect union
of word and image" whose prime concern is "the
growth of our perceptions of the world we live
in." Commenting upon the novel's unconventional
form, Larson suggests that the reader must sus-
pend "traditional concepts of the novel" when
reading *Seven Arrows*.

Larson, Charles R. "Survival of a Culture:
     Hyemeyohsts Storm's *Seven Arrows*." *The
     Novel in the Third World*. Washington,
     D.C.: Inscape Publishers, 1976, 67-88.
In the most thorough critical analysis to date of
Seven Arrows, Larson calls the novel "one of the
most extraordinary books I have ever read."
Larson dismisses criticism of the novel's inaccuracies, pointing out that it is a work of the
imagination and "not an anthropological study."
This critic carefully examines the novel's incorporation of oral materials and provides a
detailed explication of the work. He finds the
"prime achievement" of the novel to be the
"perfect union of word and image," and calls the
novel a portrayal of "not the demise of a culture
but an example of adaptability. . . ."

Larson, Charles R. *American Indian Fiction.*
Albuquerque: University of New Mexico
Press, 1978, 112-116.
In his section dealing with *Seven Arrows* in this
booklength critical study of American Indian fiction, Larson states that the story is "symbolically representative of the fate of all Indian
tribal groupings in their first encounter with
the white man." Larson discusses the two paral-
lel narratives, the "outer and inner stories,"
and suggests that the outer is "factual account
of the Plains Indians' gradual exposure to the
white man's world; the inner narrative is a much
more figurative symbolic account, told primarily
through the collective voice of the past. . . ."

Rosen, Kenneth. "American Indian Literature:
Current Condition and Suggested Research."
*American Indian Culture and Research
Journal,* 3:2 (1979), 57-66.
In this survey of contemporary American Indian
literature, Rosen observes that *Seven Arrows*
"operates on both a narrative and a metaphorical
level" and states that "*Seven Arrows* is a novel
that speaks to the need to maintain one's identity in the face of a voracious dominant culture. .
. ." Rosen concludes that "Scholarly research
into the author's relationship to his tribe may
not be particularly fruitful, but a comparison of
the fictive treatment of the Northern Cheyenne .
. . with their actual historical treatment might
reveal a great deal about Storm's talent as a
writer."

Smith, William F., Jr. "A Modern Masterpiece:
Seven Arrows." *The Midwest Quarterly,* 24:3
(Spring 1983), 229-247.
Smith defines *Seven Arrows* as "a modern vision of
a traditional world," and declares that the novel
"shows a sophisticated expansion of the understanding of history, for it contains four different types of Indian literature within its frame-
work." These four types of Indian literature
Smith identifies as the "modern fictional form,"

the "traditional oral form," "Indian oratory,"
and "the modern essay form." In an essay devoted
chiefly to plot summary, Smith points out the
aesthetic complexity of *Seven Arrows*, arguing
that the work contains four significant struc-
tural elements: the introduction, the novel's
episodic nature, the integration of traditional
Indian narratives, and the use of "arguments."

Reviews

Seven Arrows
  American Anthropologist. Volume 75, August
    1973, 1040.
  Booklist. Volume 69, January 1, 1973, 428.
  Booklist. Volume 69, January 15, 1973, 490.
  Choice. Volume 9, November 1972, 1213.
  Harpers. Volume 245, November 1972, 120.
  Kirkus Reviews. Volume 40, May 1, 1972, 571.
  Library Journal. Volume 97, July 1972, 2436.
  Library Journal. Volume 97, December 1972,
    4097.
  Natural History. Volume 81, November 1972, 96.
  Newsweek. Volume 81, January 15, 1973, 69.
  New Yorker. Volume 48, December 2, 1972, 211.
  New York Times Book Review. March 18, 1973,
    37.
  Publishers Weekly. Volume 201, May 1, 1972,
    47.
  Publishers Weekly. Volume 204, September 17,
    1973, 58.
  Saturday Review of Literature. Volume 55, July
    1, 1972, 50.
  Wall Street Journal. Volume 181, January 16,
    1973, 18.

The Song of Heyoehkah
  Booklist. Volume 77, May 15, 1981, 1242.
  Best Sellers. Volume 41, July 1981, 134.
  Kirkus Reviews. Volume 49, March 15, 1981,
    384.
  Library Journal. Volume 106, May 1, 1981, 993.
  Publishers Weekly. Volume 219, March 20, 1981,
    56.

John William Tebbel
(1912 -)

I. Biography

Perhaps the most prolific of all writers of
American Indian descent, Tebbel is of Ojibwa
ancestry and was born in Boyne City, Michigan.
He is the great-great-grandson of John Johnston
and Susan (known, according to Tebbel, as Woman
of the Green Glade and keeper of the oral tradition of the Ojibway tribe). Tebbel received a
B.A. degree from Central Michigan University and
an M.S. degree from Columbia University. During
a long career as a journalist and free-lance
writer, he has worked for such publications as
the *Detroit Free Press*, the *American Mercury*,
Newsweek, and the *New York Times* and has served
as associate editor for E.P. Dutton & Co. and as
professor of journalism and head of the journalism department at New York University. From 1958
to 1962, Tebbel directed the Graduate Institute
of Book Publishing at New York University.
Tebbel has also served as a consultant to the
Ford Foundation. In addition to three historical
novels, Tebbel has published a large number of
non-fiction books and more than five hundred
articles in popular magazines.

II. Primary Sources

Novels

The Conqueror. New York: Dutton, 1951.
This historical novel, Tebbel's first, is based
on the life of Sir William Johnson, British
superintendent-general of Indian affairs in North
America in the years before the French and Indian
War. Tebbel follows Johnson's career from his
landing in New York (from Ireland) through his
adventures as overseer of his uncle's large land
holdings along the Mohawk River and as spokesman

for the Indian Confederation. Tebbel crowds a
great deal of historical detail into this
fictional account.

Touched With Fire. New York: Dutton, 1952.
Tebbel's second historical novel is based on the
life of La Salle, after that explorer had reached
the New World. Tebbel's novel records La Salle's
adventures from Mississippi to the Canadian tun-
dra, adventures involving skirmishes with Indians, political intrigue, and general hardship.

A Voice in the Streets. New York: Dutton,
    1954.
An historical novel set in nineteenth century New
York City, this book traces the rise of a young
Irishman from poverty to wealth and power.
Tebbel incorporates generous amounts of histori-
cal facts and detail.

Other Booklength Works

*An American Dynasty: The Story of the
    McCormicks, Medills, and Pattersons*. Garden
    City: Doubleday, 1947. Reprint, Greenwood
    Press, 1968.
The Marshall Fields. New York: Dutton, 1947.
*George Horace Lorimer and the Saturday Evening
    Post*. Garden City: Doubleday, 1948.
(With Kenneth N. Stewart) *Makers of Modern
    Journalism*. Englewood Cliffs, New Jersey:
    Prentice-Hall 1950.
Your Body: How to Keep it Healthy. New
    York: Harper, 1951.
*The Life and Good Times of William Randolph
    Hearst*. New York: Dutton, 1952.
George Washington's America. New York:
    Dutton, 1954.
*The Magic of Balanced Living: A Man's Key to
    Health, Well-Being, and Peace of Mind*. New
    York: Harper, 1956.
(With Keith Jennison) *The American Indian
    Wars*. New York: Harper, 1960.

*The Inheritors: A Study of America's Great
Fortunes and What Happened to Them.* New
York: Putnam, 1962.
*The Human Touch in Business: The Story of
Charles R. Hook, Who Rose From Office Boy
to Internationally-Known Business Leader.*
Otterbein Press, 1963.
David Sarnoff: Putting Electrons to Work.
Chicago: Encyclopaedia Britannica, 1963.
Paperback Books: A Pocket History. New
York: Pocket Books, 1963.
The Compact History of the American Newspaper.
New York: Hawthorn, 1963. Revised edition,
1969.
*From Rags to Riches: Horatio Alger, Jr. and
the American Dream.* New York: Macmillan,
1964.
*Red Runs the River: The Rebellion of Chief
Pontiac.* New York: Hawthorn, 1966.
The Compact History of the Indian Wars. New
York: Hawthorn, 1966.
Open Letters to Newspaper Readers. New York:
James Heineman, 1968.
The Compact History of American Magazines. New
York: Hawthorn, 1969.
(With Ramon Eduardo Ruiz) *South by
Southwest: The Mexican-American and His
Heritage.* Garden City: Doubleday, 1969.
*The Battle of Fallen Timbers, August 20,
1774: President Washington Secures the
Ohio Valley.* New York: F. Watts, 1972.
*A History of Book Publishing in the United
States,* Volume I: *The Creation of an
Industry, 1630-1865.* New York: Bowker,
1972.
*A History of Book Publishing in the United
States,* Volume II: *The Expansion of an
Industry, 1865-1919.* New York: Bowker,
1975.
*A History of Book Publishing in the United
States,* Volume III: *The Golden Age:
Between Two Wars, 1920-1940.* New York:
Bowker, 1978.

*A History of Book Publishing in the United
States,* Volume IV: *A Great Period of
Growth: 1940-1980.* New York: Bowker,
1980.
*The Media in America: A Social and Political
History.* New York: Crowell, 1974.

Selected Shorter Publications

Articles and Essays

"AIGA: Fifty Books of 1961." *Publishers
Weekly,* 181 (May 7, 1962), 55-57.
"Amazing Communications World of Roy Thomson."
Saturday Review, 48 (October 9, 1965), 66-
68+.
"Are Authors Obsolete?" *Saturday Review,* 48
(December 11, 1965), 68-69.
"Behind the Publishing Scene." *Saturday
Review,* 46 (January 19, 1963), 15-16.
"Books Go Co-Operative." *Saturday Review,* 44
(April 15, 1961), 24-25+.
"Books in Communications." *Saturday Review,* 45
(October 13, 1962), 61.
"Book Publishers' Salvation?" *Saturday Review,*
49 (January 23, 1966), 32-33.
"Britain's Chronic Press Crisis." *Saturday
Review,* 50 (July 8, 1967), 49-50.
"Britain's Troubled Air." *Saturday Review,* 50
(August 12, 1967), 60-61.
"Broadcasting's Hidden Power: The TV-Radio
Reps." *Saturday Review,* 52 (December 13,
1969), 68-69.
"Business Magazines: A Growing Force."
Saturday Review, 51 (May 11, 1968), 69-70.
"Can Journalism Schools Improve the Press?"
Saturday Review, 53 (January 17, 1970), 63-
65.
"Century of The World Almanac." *Saturday
Review,* 50 (December 9, 1967), 62-63.
"Changing American Newsboy." *Saturday Review,*
54 (February 13, 1971), 56-58.

"Chautauqua: A Nostalgic Salute." *Saturday
Review*, 52 (January 11, 1969), 122-123.
"Chicago Tribune." *American Mercury*, 58 (March
1944), 299-307.
"Children's TV, European Style." *Saturday
Review*, 50 (February 11, 1967), 70-71+.
"City Magazines: A Medium Reborn." *Saturday
Review*, 51 (March 9, 1968), 102-103.
"Coming 3-D Revolution." *Saturday Review*, 47
(March 14, 1964), 127-128.
"Crisis for the Independent Daily." *Saturday
Review*, 46 (January 12, 1963), 94.
"Detroit, City for Victory." *American Mercury*,
54 (April 1942), 403-411.
"Do News Media Overplay Disorder? Press Power
Revisited." *Saturday Review*, 53 (June 13,
1970), 53-54.
"Editors and Publishers: A Confrontation?"
Saturday Review, 52 (July 12, 1969), 49-50.
"Electronic Composing Room: How Near Is It?"
Saturday Review, 48 (June 12, 1965), 75-76.
"Eyes and Ears of the World." *Saturday Review*,
54 (June 13, 1971), 60-62.
"Failing Newspapers and Anti-Trust Laws."
Saturday Review, 53 (December 12, 1970),
58-59.
"Fleet Street Fortune at Work: Two Seminars in
Understanding." *Saturday Review*, 49
(November 12, 1966), 101-102.
"FM: Radio's Problem Child." *Saturday Review*,
45 (January 9, 1965), 67-68.
"FM: A New Trend Toward Quality." *Saturday
Review*, 45 (May 12, 1962), 70-71.
"Forecasting the Seventies." *Saturday Review*,
52 (November 8, 1969), 80-81.
"Freedom of the Air." *Saturday Review*, 45
(April 14, 1962), 56-57.
"Global Freedom of the Press: Slow
Strangulation." *Saturday Review*, 51
(September 14, 1968), 140-141.
"Great Copying Boom." *Saturday Review*, 49 (May
14, 1966), 62-63.

"Great Media Impact War." *Saturday Review*, 50
(June 10, 1967), 96-97.
"Happiness is a Comic Strip." *Saturday Review*,
52 (April 12, 1969), 72-73+.
"Hard Sell in Washington." *Saturday Review*, 47
(July 11, 1964), 51+.
"Hardy Independent." *High Finance*, 14
(February 1964), 46-48.
"Horatio Alger Revisited: Excerpt from *From
Rags to Riches*, Horatio Alger, Jr. and the
American Dream." *Publishers Weekly*, 183
(February 18, 1963), 121-125.
"How Europe Fights Commercial TV." *Saturday
Review*, 46 (August 10, 1963), 46-47.
"How the British View Their Press." *Saturday
Review*, 45 (December 8, 1962), 68-69.
"How to Evade the Issue." *Saturday Review*, 47
(January 11, 1964), 79-80.
"Howards of Newspaper Street." *Saturday
Review*, 45 (November 10, 1962), 64-65.
"How to Review a Best-Seller." *Saturday
Review*, 44 (January 14, 1961), 39-40.
"Inside Soviet Television." *Saturday Review*,
55 (January 8, 1972), 48-49.
"It's Up in the Air: Who Owns Television?"
Saturday Review, 52 (May 10, 1969), 75-76.
"JFK, the Magazines, and Peace." *Saturday
Review*, 46 (December 14, 1963), 56-57.
"Journalism's Challenge and Answers." *Saturday
Review*, 46, (July 8, 1963), 50-51.
"Journalism Education: Myth and Reality."
Saturday Review, 48 (November 13, 1965),
92+.
"Keeping Up With Knowledge." *Saturday Review*,
48 (July 10, 1965), 52-53.
"Large-Type Books: An Expanding Horizon."
Saturday Review, 51 (July 13, 1968), 55-56.
"Leon Shimkin: The Businessman as Publisher."
Saturday Review, 49 (September 10, 1966),
74-75+.
"Libraries in Miniature: A New Era Begins."
Saturday Review, 54 (January 9, 1971), 41-
42.

"Library Week 1968: Being All You Can Be."
   Saturday Review, 51 (April 20, 1968), 24-
   25+.
"Little Giant of Nassau County." *Saturday*
   Review, 48 (February 12, 1965), 68-70.
"Long Dream of Thomas Wolf." *American Mercury*,
   53 (December 1941), 752-754.
"Magazines." *Saturday Review*, 45 (October 13,
   1962), 54-55.
"Magazines: New, Changing, Growing." *Saturday*
   Review, 52 (February 8, 1969), 55-56.
"Making the British Press Responsible."
   Saturday Review, 50 (October 14, 1967),
   118+.
"Micrographics: A Growing Industry." *Saturday*
   Review, 54 (July 10, 1971), 48-50.
"Miniaturization of the Book." *Current*, 126
   (February 1971), 46-51.
"Mitch's Biggest Pitch." *Saturday Review*, 46
   (November 9, 1963), 69-70+.
"Most Maligned Town in the U.S." *Holiday*, 11
   (February 1952), 96-97.
"Music by Mall." *High Finance*, 13 (March
   1963), 42-45+.
"Network Television's Uncertain Future."
   Saturday Review, 53 (November 14, 1970),
   69-70.
"New Life for the Cheshire Cat." *Saturday*
   Review, 48 (May 8, 1965), 64-65.
"New Look in Alumni Magazines." *Saturday*
   Review, 45 (February 10, 1962), 64-65.
"New Look at Curtis." *Saturday Review*, 49
   (June 11, 1966), 94-95+.
"New Look in Newspaper P.R." *Saturday Review*,
   44 (April 8, 1961), 55-56.
"New Trends Affecting Books and Authors."
   Publishers Weekly, 179 (March 13, 1961),
   26-27.
"*New York Times* Goes West." *Saturday Review*,
   44 (November 11, 1961), 69-71.
"Newest TV Boom: Spanish-Language Stations."
   Saturday Review, 51 (June 8, 1968), 70-71.

"Newsletters: The Ubiquitous Medium." *Saturday Review*, 48 (August 14, 1965), 57-58.

"Newspapers and the Culture Beat." *Saturday Review*, 46 (April 13, 1963), 61+.

"Old New Journalism." *Saturday Review*, 54 (March 13, 1971), 96-97.

"Our Shrinking Magazines: Time to Change Your Page Size." *Saturday Review*, 54 (October 8, 1971), 68-70.

"Papa's Troubled Legacy." *Saturday Review*, 49 (April 9, 1966), 30-31+.

"Paperbacks: Revolution or Evolution?" *Saturday Review*, 47 (June 13, 1964), 62-63.

"Paperback Textbook Revolution." *Saturday Review*, 44 (March 11, 1961), 81+.

"PBL: The Great Experiment." *Saturday Review* 50 (November 11, 1967), 85-87+.

"People and Jobs." *Saturday Review*, 50 (December 30, 1967), 8-12+.

"Picture-Man on 57th Street." *Saturday Review*, 44 (February 11, 1961), 86-87.

"Portrait." *Saturday Review of Literature*, 30 (November 29, 1947), 14.

"Presidents and the Press." *Saturday Review*, 46 (September 14, 1963), 68-70+.

"Press Under Assault." *Saturday Review*, 51 (October 12, 1968), 77-78.

"Printing Enters the Common Market." *Saturday Review*, 45 (August 11, 1962), 39-40.

"Private Mail Delivery? The Postman Rings Twice." *Saturday Review*, 52 (June 14, 1969), 50-51.

"Prospect Before Us." *Saturday Review*, 52 (April 28, 1969), 19-22.

"PR in the Advertising Agency." *Saturday Review*, 43 (November 12, 1960), 110-111.

"Publisher to an Era." *Saturday Review*, 47 (August 29, 1964), 131-133+.

"Pulitzer Idea: Fifty Years Old." *Saturday Review*, 46 (March 9, 1963), 52-53.

"Putting the *Times* to Bed." *Saturday Review*, 47 (December 12, 1964), 67-68+.

"Quiet Offset Revolution." *Saturday Review, 44
(December 9, 1961), 60-61.*
"Rating the American Newspaper." Saturday
    Review, 44 (May 13, 1954), 60-62; (June 10,
    1961), 54-56.
"Readers Digest Goes to College." *Saturday
    Review,* 50 (May 13, 1967), 92-93.
"Recruiting in the Inner City." *Saturday
    Review,* 54 (July 11, 1970), 54-55.
"Remarkable Mr. Mayes." *Saturday Review,* 43
    (October 8, 1960), 64.
"Reporting the World's Fair." *Saturday Review,*
    47 (April 11, 1964), 83-84.
"Reporting the United Nations." *Saturday
    Review,* 51 (November 9, 1968), 82-83.
"Responsibility and the Mass Media." *Saturday
    Review,* 46 (February 9, 1963), 58-59.
"Revolution in Layout." *Saturday Review,* 53
    (September 12, 1970), 93-94.
"Rise of the Talking Book." *Saturday Review,*
    44 (August 12, 1961), 42-43.
"Safeguarding U.S. History." *Saturday Review,*
    45 (June 23, 1962), 24-25+.
"Sex Education: Yesterday, Today, and
    Tomorrow." *Today's Education,* 65 (January
    1976), 70-72.
"Sigma Delta Chi's New Look." *Saturday
    Review,*   (April 8, 1967), 84+.
"Strong and Steady Light." *Saturday Review,* 48
    (March 13, 1965), 145+.
"Studying the Mass Media." *Saturday Review,* 53
    (February 14, 1970), 69-71.
"Summer of Discontent." *Saturday Review,* 52
    (September 13, 1969), 110-111.
"Teacher of the Unteachables." *Saturday
    Review,* 48 (May 15, 1965), 72+.
"Television: The View from Europe." *Saturday
    Review,* 52 (August 9, 1969), 43-44.
"TV and Radio." *New American Mercury,* 71:720-
    725; 72:201-105, 235-238 (December 1950-
    February 1951).
"They All Became Barons." *Saturday Review,* 45
    (February 24, 1962), 40.

"They Never Left Home." *Saturday Review*, 46
  (May 11, 1963), 56+.
"Thunder on the Thames." *Saturday Review*, 46
  (July 13, 1963), 44-46.
"To Europe for $100." *New American Mercury*, 71
  (December 1950), 702-706.
"Training for the Journalist in Africa and
  Vietnam." *Saturday Review*, 49 (December 10,
  1966), 84-85+.
"Twenty Years of Transistors." *Saturday
  Review*, 51 (December 14, 1968), 66-68.
"Two Hundred Years of Progress." *Saturday
  Review*, 51 (February 10, 1968), 59-60+.
"U.N.'s Hidden 85 Per Cent." *Saturday Re iew*,
  45 (February 24, 1962), 23-25.
"U.S. Television Abroad." *Saturday Review*, 45
  (July 14, 1962), 44-45.
"Wall Street Publishing Giant." *Saturday
  Review*, 51 (January 13, 1968), 110-111+.
"West Germany's Publishing Powerhouse."
  Saturday Review, 50 (January 14, 1967),
  125-126.
"What are the Journalism Schools Teaching?"
  Saturday Review, 49 (August 13, 1966), 48-
  50.
"What's Ahead in Book Publishing?" *Publishers
  Weekly*, 181 (May 28, 1962).
"What's Happening to Journalism Education?"
  Saturday Review, 46 (October 12, 1963), 52-
  53; 47 (October 10, 1964), 103-104+.
"What Happens to J-School Graduates?" *Saturday
  Review*, 50 (March 11, 1967), 126-127+.
"What's Happening to Sunday Newspapers?"
  Saturday Review, 49 (January 8, 1966), 110-
  111.
"What is Happening to UHF?" *Saturday Review*,
  51 (April 13, 1968), 89-90.
"What's Happening to the Underground Press."
  Saturday Review, 54 (November 13, 1971),
  89-90.
"What News Does the Public Believe?" *Saturday
  Review*, 45 (March 10, 1962), 43-44.

"What Tomorrow's Front Page Will Look Like."
Saturday Review, 54 (May 8, 1971), 50-52.
"When a Book Hits the Jackpot." *Saturday
Review*, 49 (February 12, 1966), 62-64.
"When Movies Joined the Jet Set." *Saturday
Review*, 47 (November 14, 1964), 78-79.
"Where are the New Recruits?" *Saturday Review*,
45 (September 8, 1962), 66-67+.
"Who Says the Comics are Read?" *Saturday
Review*, 43 (December 10, 1960), 44-46.
"Wide Open Spaces." *Saturday Review*, 45
(January 13, 1962), 73-74+.
"World Press and the Teaching of Journalism."
Saturday Review, 54 (September 11, 1971),
64-65.
"Worst-Covered Stories: What's the News?"
Saturday Review, 53 (March 14, 1970), 111-
112.

III. Selected Secondary Sources

Reviews

The Conqueror
  Chicago Sunday Tribune. April 8, 1951, 5.
  Library Journal. Volume 76, March 15, 1951,
    514.
  New York Times. April 8, 1951, 22.
  Saturday Review of Literature. Volume 34,
    April 28, 1951, 14.
  Springfield Republican. May 6, 1951, 26A.

Touched With Fire
  Chicago Sunday Tribune. June 1, 1952, 3.
  Kirkus Reviews. Volume 20, February 15, 1952,
    134.
  New York Herald Tribune Book Review. May 25,
    1952, 14.
  New York Times. April 20, 1952, 25.
  Saturday Review of Literature. Volume 35,
    August 16, 1952, 32.
  Springfield Republican. July 27, 1952, 6D.

Voice in the Streets
  Kirkus Reviews. Volume 22, June 1, 1954, 344.
  Library Journal. Volume 79, July 1954, 1311.
  New York Times. August 8, 1954, 4.
  Saturday Review of Literature. Volume 37,
      August 21, 1954, 37.

Biographical Sources

*American Authors and Books, 1640 to the
    Present Day*, 3rd rev. ed. by J. Burke and
    Will D. Howe, Rev. Irving Weiss and Anne
    Weiss. New York: Crown Publishers, 1972.
Current Biography, 1940-1976, ed. by Marjorie
    Dent Candee. New York: H.W. Wilson Co.,
    1953.
*The Foreign Press: A Survey of the World's
    Journalism.* By John C. Merrill, Carter R.
    Bryan, Marvin Alisky. Baton Rouge:
    Louisiana State University Press, 1975.
*Literature by and about the American Indian:
    An Annotated Bibliography*, ed. by Anna Lee
    Stensland. Urbana, Illinois: National
    Council of Teachers of English, 1979.
*The Literary Journal in America to 1900: A
    Guide to Information Sources.* The American
    Literature, English Literature, and World
    Literatures in English Information Guide
    Series, vol. 3. Ed. by Edward E. Whielens.
    Detroit: Gale Research Co., 1975.
Who's Who in America, 42nd ed., vol. 2 (1982-
    83). Chicago: Marquis Who's Who, Inc.

James Tucker
(1948 -   )

I. Biography

Tucker, Choctaw and Cherokee, was born in
Oklahoma City and grew up in Oklahoma and
Arizona. Tucker briefly attended college in
Arkansas and then served as a medic in Vietnam
and later as an infantry officer. He is a
graduate of Brigham Young University. The author
has written short stories, plays, and two novels:
Stone: The Birth, published in 1981, and *Stone:
The Journey*, also published in 1981. Tucker has
several works in progress, but he is currently
concentrating on finishing the third part of his
trilogy, *Stone: The Farewell*.

II. Primary Sources

Novels

Stone: The Birth. New York: Zebra Books,
       1981.
The Stone mythos is based heavily upon Cherokee
legends and deals with a period when the White
man was just appearing on the Eastern shores of
North America. As the novel opens Bear Man
marries Tree who later gives birth to Stone, the
protagonist of the Stone mythos. Bear Man kills
some members of an enemy tribe who have encroach-
ed upon his tribe's territory. Bear Man is
killed in a battle with the enemy tribe and Tree
is left to raise Stone by herself. Two witches
befriend Tree and teach her to be independent and
help her to raise Stone, whom they desire to turn
to their evil ways. Tree remarries, but Archer--
her second husband--is killed by Stone's old
friend, Crawler. Tree next marries, against
tribal custom, Light Fire, who is the band's
leader and who was Bear Man's father. Tree takes
Stone into the woods when he is twelve and leaves

him there as a rite of passage. The witches
follow Tree and try to make her tell them where
she has left Stone. Tree and Light Fire fight
with the witches and kill them. Reports of the
arrival of the White people who have been in
Light Fire's dreams make the leader fear for the
safety of his band. The Whites are attacked by
the same enemy tribe that killed Bear Man and
Light Fire's band are banished from the rest of
the tribe because they refused to go to the aid
of the White people. The enemy tribe attacks
Light Fire's band and he is killed in the battle.
Tear Maker, the daughter of one of the witches
and Stone's lover, is captured by the leader of
the enemy tribe, I Shout. Stone and Tree gather
the remnants of the band and Tree becomes Stone's
mate.

   Stone: The Journey. New York: Zebra Books,
      1981.
The Wizard, the brother of the witches in the *The
Birth*, senses that his sisters are dead and he
vows to punish Tree and her mate. While he is
hunting, Stone is badly wounded by a buck but is
brought back to health by New Human, whom Stone
met years before when he was on his rite of passage. New Human is accompanied by her daughter,
Earth, who was fathered by Stone. Dwarf, a
product of The Wizard's evil, enters the story
and vows to kill The Wizard. Tear Maker escapes
from I Shout, but he follows after her. The
Wizard saves Dwarf when he is attacked by a bear
and the pair meet Stone, New Human, and Earth who
are trying to catch up with the wandering band,
which is now lead by Tree. The Wizard decides
not to harm Stone, who, he has learned, is Tree's
son and mate. I Shout and his men attack Stone's
camp and in the battle New Human, Earth, and Tear
Maker - who has found Stone - are killed along
with I Shout and his men. Stone, The Wizard, and
Dwarf find the group led by Tree and The Wizard
decides not to harm her. In the Spring Tree dies
while giving birth to twins: Night and Day.
Stone declares that the journey must continue.

Selected Shorter Publications

Short Fiction

"The October Man." *Touchstone.* Salt Lake City:
The Mysterious Stranger Press, 1978.

"The Man Who Lived in Kaleidoscope Glass." Roy
Torgeson, ed., *Other Worlds #2.* New York:
Zebra Books, 1980.

"Alas My Love You Do Me Wrong." Orson Scott
Card, ed., *Dragons of Darkness.* New York:
Ace Books, 1981.

"The Stadium." Lois Collins, ed., *Expression,*
1:4. Salt Lake City, 1982.

"The Man in the Wall." Tony Markham, ed., *The
Leading Edge,* no. 4. Provo, Utah, 1982.

Gerald Vizenor
(1934 -)

I. Biography

Vizenor, a Chippewa enrolled at the White Earth
Reservation in Minnesota, was born in
Minneapolis. He served with the U.S. Army in
Japan and after his discharge studied at New York
University and received a B.A. degree from the
University of Minnesota. Vizenor has worked for
various state agencies in Minnesota and has been
director of Inter-Cultural Programs at Park
Rapids, Minnesota. He has also served as
director of the American Indian Employment and
Guidance Center in Minneapolis and as director of
American Indian Studies both at Bemidji State
College in Minnesota and the University of
California at Berkeley. Vizenor is currently
Professor of American Studies at the University
of Minnesota, Minneapolis, and has taught during
the 1983-84 year at Tiajin University in the
People's Republic of China.

II. Primary Sources

Novels

>   *Darkness in Saint Louis Bearheart.* Saint
>   Paul: Truck Press, 1978.

When members of the radical American Indian
Movement break into the offices of the Bureau of
Indian Affairs, a young Indian woman encounters
Saint Louis Bearheart, an old man in the Heirship
Office. After first scorning and then having sex
with the old man, the woman reads a manuscript
Bearheart has written: "Cedarfair Circus: Grave
Reports from the Cultural Word Wars."
Bearheart's book is Vizenor's novel, a story of
Proude Cedarfair, who leads a bizarre group of
Indian and non-Indian people from the sacred
ancestral Cedar Circus in Minnesota to Pueblo

125

Bonito in the southwestern U.S. The novel is set
during a future time when civilization has
collapsed due to insufficient oil supplies,
unleashing perverse and evil powers with which
the Cedarfair pilgrims must contend. In the
course of the trickster-like journey, most of the
pilgrims meet strange and violent ends.

Other Booklength Words

Poems Born in the Wind. Copyright by the
    author, 1960.
The Old Park Sleepers. Copyright by the
    author, 1961.
Two Wings the Butterfly. Copyright by the
    author, 1962
South of the Painted Stones. Minneapolis:
    Nodin Press, 1963.
Raising the Moon Vines. Minneapolis: Nodin
    Press, 1964.
Seventeen Chirps; Haiku in English.
    Minneapolis: Nodin Press, 1964.
*Summer in the Spring; Lyric Poems of the
    Ouibway.* Minneapolis: Nodin Press, 1965.
*Slight Abrasions: A Dialogue with Jerome
    Downers.* Minneapolis: Nodin Press, 1966.
Empty Swings; Haiku in English. Minneapolis:
    Nodin Press, 1967.
*Escorts to the White Earth, 1868-1968: One
    Hundred Years on a Reservation.*
    Minneapolis: Four Winds Press, 1968.
Thomas James Whitehawk. Minneapolis: Four
    Winds Press, 1968.
anishinabe adisokan: Tales of the People.
    Minneapolis: The Nodin Press, 1970.
anishinabe nagomon: Songs of the People.
    Minneapolis: The Nodin Press, 1970.
*The Everlasting Sky: New Voices from the
    People Named the Chippewa.* New York:
    Crowell-Collier Press, 1972.
Tribal Scenes and Ceremonies. (A collectin of
    editorials, news articles, and magazine
    stories). Minneapolis: Nodin Press, 1976.

*Wordarrows: Indians and Whites in the New Fur
      Trade.* Minneapolis: University of
      Minnesota Press, 1978.
*Summer in the Spring: Ouibwe Lyric Poems and
      Tribal Stories.* Minneapolis: Nodin Press,
      1981.
*Earthdivers: Tribal Narratives of Mixed
      Descent.* Minneapolis: University of
      Minnesota Press, 1981.

Selected Shorter Publications

Poems

"Anishinabe Grandmothers." In *Voices of the
      Rainbow: Contemporary Poetry by American
      Indians.* Kenneth Rosen, ed. New York:
      Seaver Books, 1975, 44.
"Auras on the Interstate." In *Songs From This
      Earth on Turtle's Back: Contemporary
      American Indian Poetry.* Joseph Bruchac, ed.
      Greenfield Center, New York: Greenfield
      Review Press, 1983, 265-266.
"Creation Fires." *Moons and Lion Tailes,* 2:4,
      1978, 49.
"Family Photograph." In Rosen, *Voices of the
      Rainbow,* 37.
"Fathers of My Breath." In Tvedten, Benet,
      comp., *An American Indian Anthology.*
      Marvin, S.D.: Blue Cloud Abbey, 1971, 45.
"February Park." In Rosen, *Voices of the
      Rainbow,* 33.
"Haiku." In *From The Belly of the Shark: A New
      Anthology of Native Americans.* Walter
      Lowenfelds, ed. New York: Vintage Books,
      1973, 69. Reprint in Rosen, *Voices of the
      Rainbow,* 39.
"Holiday Inn at Bemidui." In Bruchac, *Songs
      From This Earth On Turtle's Back,* 266.
"Indians at the Guthrie." In Rosen, *Voices of
      the Rainbow,* 31. Reprinted in Bruchac,
      Songs From This Earth on Turtle's Back,
      264.

"Long After the Rivers Change." In Tvedten,
    Benet, comp., *An American Indian Anthology.*
    Marvin, S.D.: Blue Cloud Abbey, 1971, 46.
"Love Poems and Spring Poems and Dream Poems
    and War Poems" (translated from the
    Anishinabe by Vizenor). In *The Way: An
    Anthology of American Indian Literature.*
    Shirley Hill Witt and Stan Steiner, eds.
    New York: Alfred A. Knopf, 1972, 134-137.
"Minnesota Camp Grounds." In Bruchac, *Songs
    From This Earth on Turtle's Back,* 265.
"The Moon Upon A Face Again." In Tvedten,
    Benet, comp., *An American Indian Anthology.*
    Marvin, S.D.: Blue Cloud Abbey, 1971, 47.
"North to Milwaukee." In Rosen, *Voices of the
    Rainbow,* 42.
"An Old Spider Web." In Tvedten, Benet, comp.,
    An American Indian Anthology. Marvin, S.D.:
    Blue Cloud Abbey, 1971, 48.
"Poems: The Sky Clears; Concerning a Brave
    Woman; Mide Initiation Song; Song of
    Spring." *Sun Tracks,* 1 (June, 1971), 10-11.
"Raising the Flag." In Rosen, *Voices of the
    Rainbow,* 42.
"Seven Woodland Crows." In Rosen, *Voices of
    the Rainbow,* 43.
"Six Haiku Poems: California 1978." *Chariton
    Review,* 5:1, (Spring 1979), 67.
"Thumbing Old Magaznes." In Rosen, *Voices of
    the Rainbow,* 36.
"Tribal Stumps." In Rosen, *Voices of the
    Rainbow,* 32.
"Tropisms on John Berryman." In Rosen, *Voices
    of the Rainbow,* 34.
"Tyranny of Moths." In Rosen, *Voices of the
    Rainbow,* 35.
"Unhapppy Diary Days." In Rosen, *Voices of the
    Rainbow,* 32.
"White Earth Reservation." In Bruchac, *Songs
    From This Earth on Turtle's Back,* 262-263.

Short Fiction

"Manabozho and the Gambler." In Witt and
    Steiner, *The Way*, 53-55.
"Rattling Hail Ceremonial: Cultural Word Wars
    Downtown on the Reservation." *Shantih*, 4:2
    (Summer-Fall 1979), 40-41.
"Songs of the People (Anishinabe Nagamon)." In
    *The Way: An Anthology of American Indian
    Literature*. Shirley Hill Witt and Stan
    Steiner, eds. New York: Alfred A. Knopf,
    1972, 33-38.

Articles and Essays

"I Know What You Mean, Erdupps MacChurbbs:
    Autobiographical Myths and Metaphors."
    *Growing Up in Minnesota: Ten Writers
    Remember Their Childhoods*. Chester
    Andersen, ed. Minneapolis: University of
    Minnesota Press, 1976, 79-111.
"The Pretend Indians." *Film Quarterly*, 34
    (Summer 1981), 36.

III. Selected Secondary Sources

Criticism of *Darkness in Saint Louis Bearheart*

Hunter, Carol. "American Indian Literature.
    MELUS, 8:2 (Summer 1981), 82-85.
In this brief essay, Hunter divides American
Indian literature into the categories of traditional oral literature and modern fiction and
asserts that "American Indian writers of the
1980's project tribal ethos, regional identity,
and their cultural heritage" from the traditional
oral literature. Hunter points out that in
Darkness in Saint Louis Bearheart Vizenor has
used "oral literature from a wide variety of
mythical episodes and characters."

Velie, Alan R. *Four American Indian Literary
   Masters*. Norman: University of Oklahoma
   Press, 1982, 126-37.
In the most comprehensive criticism to date on
Vizenor's fiction, Velie provides a general
introduction to the author and his works and
attempts to place *Darkness in Saint Louis
Bearheart* in the contemporary post-modernist
movement. Velie examines the significance of the
trickster and sacred clown figures in Indian
tradition and religion and in Vizenor's novel,
and he states that "at the heart of the book is
an ever-present and peculiarly Indian sense of
humor."

Reviews of *Darkness in Saint Louis Bearheart*

American Indian Culture and Research Journal.
   Volume 4, 1980, 187-191.
Library Journal. Volume 103, December 15,
   1978, 2486.
Library Journal. Volume 104, January 1, 1979,
   130.
Talking Leaf: Los Angeles Indian Newspaper.
   No. 9, September 1983, 48.

Biographical Sources

Contemporary Authors. Vols. 13-14. Detroit:
   Gale Research Co., 1975.
A Directory of American Poets. New York: Poets
   and Writers, Inc., 1975.

James Welch
(1940 -)

I. Biography

Welch, Blackfeet and Gros Ventre, was born in
Browning, Montana, the headquarters and trade
center of the Blackfeet Reservation. He attended
schools at the Blackfeet and Fort Belknap Reser-
vations, until his family moved to Minneapolis.
He attended Minnesota University and Northern
Montana College and received a B.A. from the
University of Montana. He taught there for two
years in the Creative Writing Program before
leaving teaching to devote his full time to
writing. Welch's collection of poetry, *Riding
the Earthboy 40*, was published in 1971. His
novel *Winter in the Blood* was published in 1974,
and his novel *The Death of Jim Loney* was published in 1979. In addition to working as a
writer and as a teacher, Welch has also worked as
a firefighter and as an Upward Bound counselor.

II. Primary Sources

Novels

> *Winter in the Blood.* New York: Harper and
> Row, 1974. Paperback reprint New York:
> Harper and Row, (Perennial Library), 1981.
The unnamed narrator of this, Welch's first
novel, is frozen in time in his Montana waste-
land, haunted by the deaths of his brother, Mose,
and his father, First Raise, and cut off from
both his Indian heritage and the white world he
inhabits. In *Winter in the Blood*, Welch exploits
the techniques of surrealism and black humor to
underscore the young Blackfeet narrator's alienation and agony as he searches both for the Cree
girl who has jilted him and taken his gun and
razor and, more importantly, for a sense of
identity and meaning. After an absurd encounter

with the mysterious "airplane man," the narrator
finally learns that old, blind Yellow Calf, who
lives alone in a shack near the narrator's
mother's ranch, is his true grandfather, and
through Yellow Calf he is allowed a glimpse of
the older Indian world of order and meaning. In
the novel's final episode, the narrator and his
step-father, Lame Bull, bury the narrator's
grandmother in a darkly comic funeral scene and
the novel ends as the narrator throws his grandmother's tobacco pouch into the undersized grave.

The Death of Jim Loney. New York: Harper and
    Row, 1979. Paperback reprint New York:
    Harper and Row (Perennial Library), 1981.
Jim Loney is a half-breed whose days drift by as
he sits in his Harlem, Montana, kitchen with
cheap wine, an old dog, and confused visions of
departed parents and vanished relations. Loney
is trapped between Indian and white worlds, and
no one can seem to rescue him from his alienation, although Rhea, Loney's blonde lover from
Dallas, and Kate, Loney's successful bureaucrat
sister, make futile attempts to do so. During a
hunt, Loney--blinded by the sun--mistakes his one
remaining friend, Myron Pretty Weasel, for a bear
and kills him. While temporarily fleeing from
the consequences of the killing, Loney visits his
white father who fails to provide Loney with any
insight into who he is or where he comes from.
In the end, Loney goes to Mission Canyon with his
father's shotgun and waits for the Indian and
white policemen who will kill him.

Other Booklength Works

Riding the Earthboy 40. New York: World
    Publishing Company, 1971. Reprints, New
    York: Harper and Row, 1975. New York:
    Harper and Row, 1976.

Selected Shorter Publications

Poems

"Across to the Peloponnese." *American Poetry Review*, 2:6, (N-D 1973), 28. Reprinted in *Carriers of the Dream Wheel: Contemporary Native American Poetry*. Duane Niatum, ed. New York: Harper & Row, Publishers, 1975, 237, and in *Modern Poetry of Western America*. Clinton F. Larson and William Stafford, eds. Provo, Utah: Brigham Young University, 1975, 211.

"Arizona Highways." *Concerning Poetry*, 4:1, (Spring 1971), 40. Reprinted in *Carriers of the Dream Wheel: Contemporary Native American Poetry*. Duane Niatem, ed. New York: Harper & Row, Publishers, 1975, 240-241.

"Birth on Range 18." In *The American Indian Speaks*. John R. Milton, ed. Vermillion, S.D.: University of South Dakota Press, 1969, 30.

"Birthday in Sartoris." *Iowa Review*, 4:4, (Autumn 1973), 108. reprinted in *Settling America: The Ethnic Expression of 14 Contemporary Poets*. David Kherdian, ed. New York: MacMillan, 1974, 110.

"Blackfeet, Blood and Piegan Hunters." In *Young American Poets*. Paul Carroll, ed. New York: Big Table Publishing Co., 1968, 499-500. Reprinted in Kherdian, *Settling America*, 104.

"Blue Like Death." In Niatum, *Carriers of the Dream Wheel*, 235.

"Call to Arms." In Kherdian, *Settling America*, 110. Reprinted in Larson and Stafford, *Modern Poetry of Western America*, 214.

"Christmas Comes to Moccasin Flat." *Poetry Northwest*. 8 (Spring 1967), 34-35. Reprinted in Carroll, *Young American Poets*, 495-496; in *Since Feeling is First*. James Mecklenberger and Gary Simmons, eds.

Glenview, Illinois: Scott, Foresman & Co.,
1971, 19; and in *The American Indian, the
First Victim.* Jay David, ed. New York:
Morrow, 1972, 150-151. Also in *Messages.*
X.J. Kennedy, ed. Boston: Little, Brown &
Co., 1973, 145; in *The Portable North
American Indian Reader.* Frederick W.
Turner, III. New York: Viking, 1974, 597-
598; in Kherdian, *Settling America,* 105; in
Niatum, *Carriers of the Dream Wheel,* and in
Larson and Stafford, *Modern Poetry of
Western America,* 214-215.

"D-Y Bar." In Carroll, *Young American Poets,*
496-497. Reprinted in Niatum, *Carriers of
the Dream Wheel,* 250, and in *Songs From
This Earth on Turtle's Back: Contemporary
American Indian Poetry.* Joseph Bruchac, ed.
Greenfield Center, New York: The Greenfield
Review Press, 1983, 269.

"Dancing Man." *Harper's Bazaar,* 103 (August
1970), 156.

"Directions to the Nomad." *The American
Review,* 14 (1972), 114. Reprinted in
Niatum, *Carriers of the Dream Wheel,* 253.

"Dreaming with Others." *Unicorn Journal,* 4,
1972, 34.

"Dreaming Winter." *Poetry,* 112 (April 1968),
16. Reprinted in *Voices From Wah'Kon-tah:
Contemporary Poetry of Native Americans.*
Robert K. Dodge and Joseph B. McCullough,
eds. New York: International Publishers,
1974, 125.

"Flies." *Iowa Review,* 4:4 (Autumn 1973), 109.

"Getting Things Straight." In *From the Belly
of the Shark: A New Anthology of Native
Americans.* Walter Lowenfelds, ed. New York:
Vintage Books, 1973, 70.

"Going to Remake This World." In Kherdian,
Settling America, 109. Reprinted in Niatum,
Carriers of the Dream Wheel, 246.

"Grandma's Man." In Milton, *The American
Indian Speaks,* 33. Reprinted in *Forgotten
Pages of American Literature.* Gerald W.

Haslam, ed. Boston: Houghton Mifflin Co.,
   1970, 48-49.
"Gravely." In Larson and Stafford, *Modern
   Poetry of Western America*, 215.
"The Great American Poem." *Antaeus*, 32 (Winter
   1979), 82-86.
"Harlem, Montana: Just Off the Reservation."
   Poetry, 112 (April 1968), 17-18. Reprinted
   in Kherdian, *Settling America*, 107; in
   Dodge and McCulloug, *Voices From Wah'Kon-
   tah*, 126; in Niatum, *Carriers of the Dream
   Wheel*, 242-243; and in Bruchac, *Songs From
   This Earth On Turtle's Back*, 268.
"In My First Hard Springtime." *Poetry
   Northwest*, 8 (Spring 1967), 34. Reprinted
   in Carroll, *Young American Poets*, 495; in
   Niatum, *Carriers of the Dream Wheel*, 238;
   and in Larson and Stafford, *Modern Poetry
   of Western America*, 213.
"In My Lifetime." *New American Review*, no. 4.
   New York: New American Library, 1968, 162-
   163. Reprinted in *Literature of the
   American Indian*. Thomas E. Sanders and
   Walter W. Peek, eds. New York: Glencoe
   Publishing, 1973, 469; in Turner, *The
   Portable North American Indian Reader*, 598;
   in Niatum, *Carriers of the Dream Wheel*,
   245; and in Bruchac, *Songs From This Earth
   on Turtle's Back*, 271.
"In the American Express Line." *Iowa Review*,
   4:4 (Autumn 1973), 109.
"Laughing in the Belly." *Unicorn Journal*, 4
   (1972), 36.
"Legends Like This." In Milton, *The American
   Indian Speaks*, 31.
"Magic Fox." In Niatum, *Carriers of the Dream
   Wheel*, 251.
"The Man from Washington." In Milton, *The
   American Indian Speaks*, 27. Reprinted in *An
   American Indian Anthology*. Benet Tvedten,
   ed. Marvin, S.D.: Blue Cloud Abbey, 1971,
   38; in *American Indian Authors*, Natachee
   Scott Momaday, ed. Boston: Houghton

Mifflin, Co., 1972, 132; in *The Way: An Anthology of American Literature.* Shirley H. Witt, ed. New York: Knopf, 1972, 139, in Kherdian, *Settling America*, 103; in Dodge and McCullough, *Voices from Wah'Kon-tah*, 123; and in Niatum, *Carriers of the Dream Wheel*, 248.

"Meeting." *Kansas Quarterly*, 2:16 (1978), 10.

"Montana, Nothing Like Boston." In Carroll, *Young American Poets*, 498.

"One More Time." In Milton, *The American Indian Speaks*, 29. Reprinted in Dodge and McCullougm *Voices From Wah'Kon-tah*, 124.

"The Only Bar in Dixon." *New Yorker*, 46 (October 10, 1970), 48.

"Please Forward." *American Poetry Review*, 2:6 (N-D 1973), 28. Reprinted in Niatum, *Carriers of the Dream Wheel*, 244.

"Plea to Those Who Matter." In Kherdian, *Settling America*, 107.

"The Renegade Wants Words." In Kherdian, *Settling America*, 111. Reprinted in Niatum, *Carriers of the Dream Wheel*, 236.

"Response." *Shenandoah*, 3:17 (Spring 1978), 29.

"Snow Country Weavers." In Milton, *The American Indian Speaks*, 28. Reprinted in Haslam, *Forgotten Pages of American Literature*, 47, and in Sanders and Peek, *Literature of the American Indian*, 470, and in Niatum, *Carriers of the Dream Wheel*, 249.

"Spring for All Seasons." In Carroll, *Young American Poets*, 497. reprinted in Kherdian, *Settling America*, 109.

"Surviving." In Milton, *The American Indian Speaks*, 32. Reprinted in Haslam, *Forgotten Pages of American Literature*, 48, in Turner, *The Portable North American Indian Reader*, 597, in Kherdian, *Settling America*, 106, in Niatum, *Carriers of the Dream Wheel*, 239, and in Bruchac, *Songs From This Earth on Turtle's Back*, 270.

"These Are Silent Legends." *New American
Review*, no. 4. New York: New American
Library, 1968, 163.
"Verifying the Dead." *American Poetry Review*,
2:6 (N-D 1973), 28. Reprinted in Niatum,
Carriers of the Dream Wheel, 254.
"The Versatile Historian." *New American
Review*, no. 4. New York: New American
Library, 1968, 162. Reprinted in Sanders
and Peek, *Literature of the American
Indian*, 470, and in Kherdian, *Settling
America*, 105.
"Weekend Trip to the Big Hole Country."
Unicorn Journal, 4 (1972), 37.
"Why I Didn't Go To Delphi." *American Poetry
Review*, 2:6 (N-D 1973), 28. Reprinted in
Niatum, *Carriers of the Dream Wheel*, 252.
"Winter Indian." In Carroll, *Young American
Poets*, 498-499.
"Wolf Song, the Rain." In Carroll, *Young
American Poets*, 501.
"The Wrath of Lester Lame Bull." In Carroll,
Young American Poets, 500.

Short Fiction

"The Only Good Indian, Section I of a Novel in
Progress." *South Dakota Review*, 9 (1971),
55-74.

Interviews

"James Welch: Finding His Own Voice." *Four
Winds*, 156 (Spring 1980), 35.

III. Selected Secondary Sources

Criticism of *Winter in the Blood*

Allen, Paula Gunn. "A Stranger in My Own
Life: Alienation in American Indian Prose
and Poetry." *MELUS*, 7:2 (Summer 1980), 3-
19.

Allen suggests that a preoccupation with the
process of alienation is central to contemporary
American Indian writing. In a discussion of such
writers as Welch, Leslie Silko, and N. Scott
Momaday, Allen finds that alienation is characteristic of the life of the Indian "half or mixed
blood." She asserts that the nameless narrator
in *Winter in the Blood* " is adrift in a life that
lacks shape, goal, understanding, or significance. In the end, it is his recognition of this
that leads him through his impasse and allows him
to reintegrate his personality around realistic
perceptions of himself and the reality he
inhabits."

Barnett, Louise K. "Alienation and Ritual in
  *Winter in the Blood." American Indian
  Quarterly*, 4 (1978), 123-30.
The author argues that the cause of the narrator's alienation stems from the fact that he, as
an Indian, is an outcast from mainstream American
culture. Barnett traces the way that the narrator counters this alienation through personal
ritual. After a discussion of rituals in modern
society, the critic asserts that the narrator's
personal rituals take the form of remembering the
past. By the end of the novel the critic feels
that "the ritual of memory has put the narrator
in touch with what is vital and affirming in his
heritrage and given him new resolution to carry
on with his life." In addition to Barnett's
primary thesis, she provides a detailed analysis
of the work's title and also deals with what she
feels is Welch's commentary on Hemingway's "Big
Two-Hearted River."

Barry, Nora Baker. *"Winter in the Blood* as
  Elegy." *American Indian Quarterly*, 4
  (1978), 149-57.
The critic states, "Welch's novel draws not only
on the elegiac traditions of Western literature,
but also on elegiac traditions from American
Indian literature." Barry suggests that the

themes used to structure Old English elegies are
also found in the novel: the Ruin theme, the
Wanderer or Exile theme, the Last Survivor theme,
and the Funeral theme. The author traces the
forms that these themes take in the work. In her
discussion of American Indian elements which
Welch relies upon, the author deals with the
Blackfeet tale, "The Lost Woman," and with
traditional bird motifs.

   Beidler, Peter G. and Ruoff, LaVonne A.   "A
      Discussion of *Winter in the Blood*."
      American Indian Quarterly, 4 (1978), 159-
      68.
This article is an edited transcript of a discussion which followed the presentation of six
papers on *Winter in the Blood* delivered in
Chicago in 1977 at the national conference of the
Modern Language Association. The audience who
had listened to the six papers were given an
opportunity to question the panelists and to
express their own views. Various issues were
raised. First, it was argued that *Winter in the
Blood* is neither comedy nor tragedy, but walks a
fine line between the two. Next there were discussions as to the importance of the twins in the
novel and the airplane man's function in the
work. These discussions were followed by an
analysis of how Indian students have reacted to
the work. Finally the question was raised concerning the appropriateness of Anglo critics
dealing by Anglo critical means with a non-Anglo
work.

   Beidler, Peter G.   "Animals and Human
      Development in the Contemporary American
      Indian Novel." *Western American
      Literature*, 14 (Summer 1979), 133-48.
Beidler argues that *House Made of Dawn* (1966) by
N. Scott Momaday; *Winter in the Blood* (1974) by
Welch; and *Ceremony* (1977) by Leslie Silko, all
tell the same story. In each work an alienated
Indian hero drifts about until, recognizing mean-

ingful analogies between himself and the animals
around him, he puts himself in touch with their
lives and finds his proper place in the modern
world. Beidler traces Welch's narrator's sub-
jective use of animal parallelism and his
eventual awareness that he must listen to the
voices of the animals. The critic argues that
the end of the novel is positive. Referring to
the work's epigraph, Beidler asserts that the
narrator is the "bad beginner" who listened too
long to the "bones," his dead father and brother.
At the novel's conclusion, the narrator is
listening instead to the living, the animals, and
now, "there is a warmth of spring in his
blood...."

Beidler, Peter G. "Preface: A Special
    Symposium Issue." *American Indian
    Quarterly*, 4 (1978), 93-96.
Beidler presents an overview of the *American
Indian Quarterly* special issue on Welch's *Winter
in the Blood*. The articles were all delivered
first at a Modern Language Association seminar on
Welch's first novel. Although many proposals
never were chosen for the MLA presentation,
Beidler still groups the larger mass of paper
topics into four areas: "Welch's use of imagery,
the 'Indianess' of the novel, Welch's use of
Blackfoot myths, and the possibilities reflected
for human development as reflected in *Winter in
the Blood*." The articles in the special issue
deal with two issues: "the dominant emotional
condition of the narrator--his alienation" and
the tone of the novel. The critic notes that
most of the articles in the issue suggest that
"the narrator in *Winter in the Blood* does grow,
and that he has achieved a measure of wisdom by
the end of the novel."

Bell, Robert C. "Circular Design in
    Ceremony." *American Indian Quarterly*, 5
    (1979), 47-62.

James Welch   141

Although Bell deals primarily with Silko's novel,
he also discusses *Winter in the Blood*. Bell
suggests that "the pastness of the past, the
sense of loss and the remoteness of supernatural
aid, are reflected in and embody the fragmented
narrative method." The critic feels that the
sharp divisions Welch imposes on his material are
an integral, formalized part of the novel's
meaning.

   Buller, Galen. "New Interpretations of Native
       American Literature: A Survival
       Technique." *American Indian Culture and
       Research Journal*, 4:1-2 (1980), 165-77.
Buller argues that "American Indian literature is
something unique, and, as such, should be taught
as something distinctive from American literature
written by non-Indian authors." Buller points
out that Indian literature differs from the
larger body of American literature in five critical areas: "a reverence for words, a sense of
place and dependence on that sense, a feeling for
a sense of ritual, an affirmation of the need for
community, and a significantly different world-
view." Buller explains that some of his Indian
students do not accept *Winter in the Blood* as
Indian literature. Buller states that his purpose is "not to be critical of *Winter in the
Blood*." He asserts, though, that in looking at
Indian literature "as being something more, something with a unique philosophy, background and
purpose, we are allowed to make distinctions
between American Indian literature and literature
written in American by Indian authors."

   Espey, David B. "Endings in Contemporary
       American Indian Fiction." *Western American
       Literature*, 13 (Summer 1978), 133-39.
Espey refers to Frank Kermode's *The Sense of an
Ending: Studies in the Theory of Fiction* and
Vine Deloria's *God is Red* to build a case that
the Indian view of time is cyclical instead of
linear. The critic argues that Indians tradi-

tionally were not concerned with death, but
contemporary Indian writers do not share that
lack of concern due to the death of much of
Indian culture. Espey feels that Welch's novel
is representative of this modern concern of
Indians with death. The author feels that the
narrator's inability to accept traditional reli-
gious beliefs, which he says has been misread as
"existential," is representative of the breakdown
of traditional Indian values. Espey views the
funeral scene as a travesty "which attests to the
loss of an Indian cultural response to death, and
an aesthetically appropriate end for a novel in
which the Indian past is essentially dead itself." Espey feels that the narrator's movements
within the novel parody the whole meaning of
cycle: "He goes from home to bar to women and
back home again. He goes in circles; he goes
nowhere."

Horton, Andrew. "The Bitter Humor of *Winter
in the Blood*." *American Indian Quarterly*,
4 (1978), 131-39.
In this article the critic examines the various
uses Welch makes of humor in his work. Horton
primarily views the narrator as a "trickster"
figure and provides an explanation of that term,
as well as acquainting his reader with Indian
comic ceremony dramas. Although the critic views
the majority of the humor in the novel as "bitter
and ironic rather than funny in a pure comic
sense," he argues that the narrator's realization
that Yellow Calf is actually his grandfather con-
stitutes a comic epiphany during which "he experiences the healing power of the kind of laughter
Indian comic ceremony dramas evoked." Unlike
many other critics, Horton states that no clear
catharsis takes place in the narrative, and that
the narrator's humor remains bitter due to his
inability to close the distance "within himself
and between himself and others enough to see the
punch lines."

Jahner, Elaine. "Quick Paces and a Space of
    Mind." *Denver Quarterly*, 14:4 (Winter
    1980), 34-47.
The author states that some critics have failed
to acknowledge the work's stylistic complexity
because they have failed to recognize the
meanings established by the novel's several image
patterns. Jahner asserts that these patterns
are: "art as a means of traversing distance
(presented as distance and dream imagery), wind
as a life-support system (presented through wind
imagery), and alienation as a consequence of
Anglo domination (presented through winter imagery)." The critic explains the meanings of
these basic image patterns in the novel by
tracing the way the images function in Welch's
poems.

Kunz, Don. "Lost in the Distance of Winter:
    James Welch's *Winter in the Blood*."
    Critique, 20:1 (1978), 93-99.
The critic argues that *Winter in the Blood* is a
novel in which the nameless protagonist's search
for an authentic and meaningful sense of being in
the world is structured around various distances." Kunz suggests that these "various
distances" take three forms: physical, emotional, and aesthetic. The way that these forms
function within the novel is traced by the critic. Kunz also draws parallels between the way
images are parcelled out in the text and the
technique of pointillist painting. The critic
also suggests another level of meaning to the
work's title: "Doagie, whom he thinks might be
his grandfather might be the one who put the
bleakness of whiteness, the winter, in his
blood."

Larson, Charles R. *American Indian Fiction*,
    Albuquerque: University of New Mexico
    Press, 1978.
Larson notes that the opening chapters of Welch's
novel appeared years before the entire work was

published--"The Only Good Indian, Section I of a
Novel in Progress," *South Dakota Review* 9 (1971),
55-74--and that it is possible to examine the extensive revision the novel underwent. The critic
provides a summary of the events of the novel in
chronological sequence, and analyzes the work's
style and tone.

> Lattin, Vernon E. "The Quest for Mythic
>   Vision in Contemporary Native American and
>   Chicano Fiction." *American Literature*, 50:4
>   (January 1979), 625-640.

In an essay dealing mostly with Anaya and
Momaday, Lattin sees *Winter in the Blood* as very
optimistic. The narrator finds the sacred center
by questing back "to discover his grandparents
and an older vision." He sees the cow and mud
scene as the narrator's entombment and symbolic
rebirth. He sees the narrator's act of throwing
the tobacco pouch and arrowhead into the grave as
an affirmation of "the pagan vision of the con-
tinuity of life." The narrator "rediscovers the
sacred in the secular modern world."

> Lincoln, Kenneth. "Back-tracking James
>   Welch." *MELUS*, 6 (Spring 1979), 23-40.

In an article which discusses a great deal of
Welch's poetry, as well as *Winter in the Blood*,
the critic argues that "the key to Welch's art
seems an adversary's sense of reality--attitudes
that resist, counter, and invert a conventional
position in the world." Lincoln explains that
the ethnologist, Clark Wissler, records that one
of the earliest Blackfeet creation parables about
Old Man (Na'pi) and Old Woman (Kipitaki) tells
the story of wedded contraries. The critic
evaluates the novel in terms of this parable.
Lincoln then deals with Welch's surrealist
imagery, drawing parallels to the work of the
Lakota painter Oscar Howe, and also discusses
ways that the plot is structured around seven,
the Blackfeet mystic number. Finally the critic
analyzes Welch's use of color in his novel.

> Lincoln, Kenneth. *Native American Renaissance.*
> Berkeley, CA: University of California
> Press, 1983, 148-164.

After providing background on Welch and the
Blackfeet people, Lincoln devotes several pages
to a discussion of *Winter in the Blood.* The
critic states that there is a link between the
Blackfeet legend of Old Man (Na'pi) and Old Woman
(Kipitaki) and Welch's novel. Lincoln also
explains the significance of the number "seven"
to the Blackfeet and traces the function of that
number in *Winter in the Blood.* Lincoln believes
that the key to Welch is "an adversary sense of
reality--attitudes that resist, counter, and
invert conventions."

> Owens, Louis. "The Absurd Indian: Humor in the
> Novels of James Welch." *The Language of
> Humor the Humor of Language.* (Proceedings
> of the 1982 WHIM Conference). Edited by Don
> L. Nilsen; Co-editor, Alleen Pace Nilsen.
> 1983, 140-143.

In this discussion of *Winter in the Blood* and *The
Death of Jim Loney,* Owens examines the comic elements in both novels. This critic states that
Welch makes use of surrealism and black humor to
depict the absurdity of contemporary Indian existence, an absurdity which stems from Indians'
lack of harmony with their heritage and history.
Owens examines comic scenes in both of Welch's
novels and argues that the works protest the
conditions of modern Indian life: "They protest
the role of the Indian as the victim of absurd if
sometimes comical chance on a 'great earth of
stalking white men.'"

> Rhodes, Geri. "Winter in the Blood." *A: a
> journal of contemporary literature,* 4:2
> (Fall 1979), 10-17, (revision of "*Winter in
> the Blood*--Bad Medicine in the Blood." *New
> America,* 2 (Summer 1976), 44-49.)

Rhodes asserts that the novel is representative
of C.G. Jung's metaphor--the shadow side of reci-

procity. The critic states that Jung sees one of
the functions of the unconscious as compensatory
to consciousness; and if conscious is one-sided,
unconscious and opposite impulses of inferiority-
-personified as the "shadow"--will arise to coun-
terbalance the conscious attitude. Rhodes
explains that Jung believes that the shadow,
regarded as unattractive and therefore rejected
or repressed by the ego, is projected onto "suitable hooks" on the outside. The critic contends
that the narrator has many suitable hooks: the
spinster cow; his mother, whom he identifies with
the cow; women, whom he identifies with his
mother; and "this greedy stupid country," the
country of white men. Rhode feels that by trying
to save the cow, the narrator is able to integrate the shadow and, although unable to trans-
form it, is able to accept it as "bad medicine in
the blood."

    Ruoff, A. LaVonne. "Alienation and the Female
        Principle in *Winter in the Blood*."
        American Indian Quarterly, 4 (1978), 107-
        122.
Ruoff's hypothesis is that the narrator's
alienation is caused by "the distance he feels
from females in the novel--human and animal."
Ruoff traces, within her article, the narrator's
relationship with every major and minor human
female character found in the work. In addition,
Ruoff provides a great deal of insight into
Welch's use of various Blackfeet myths and taboos
and also documents the importance of the
inclusion of several animals in the work: Amos
the duck, and the cow and calf.

    Ruoff, A. LaVonne. "History in *Winter in the
        Blood*: Backgrounds and Bibliography."
        American Indian Quarterly, 4 (1978), 169-
        72.
Ruoff provides a good deal of historical informa-
tion about various tribes mentioned in the novel.
She states that there is a great deal of

confusion about the term "Blackfeet" and explains
that the Blackfeet in the novel are actually
Piegans. The critic also explains the basis for
the animosity toward Crees in the work: Cree
contact with whites, which "contrasted sharply
with the ferocity with which the Blackfeet
opposed them"; and past armed conflict which took
place between Crees and Blackfeet.

Sands, Kathleen M. "Alienation and Broken
    Narrative in *Winter in the Blood*."
    American Indian Quarterly, 4 (1978), 97-
    105.
The article argues that the narrator of *Winter in
the Blood* is alienated because "he has lost the
story of who he is, where he came from." The
critic reviews the structure of the novel and
points out how several broken narratives within
the work increase the narrator's sense of disori-
entation and alienation. Sands ultimately deals
with narratives in the novel which do "come
together," and suggests that these passages
provide the narrator with "knowledge and insight
into the past, a painful acceptance of the
present, and maybe, just maybe, the strength and
understanding to build a future."

Smith, William F. Jr. "*Winter in the Blood*:
    The Indian Cowboy as Everyman." *Michigan
    Academician*, no. 2, (Fall 1977), 299-306.
Smith argues that Welch combines the forms of the
Western and detective novel to develop a work
which deals with the most universal elements of
existence. The critic states, "*Winter in the
Blood* shows us an unnamed narrator facing the
basic mysteries of life and death, solving them
to the best of his ability, and then living the
life he has. This is the fundamental pattern
that every adult must face, a pattern of Every-
man." It is the pattern of the detective novel
which Smith uses chiefly to analyze Welch's
work. Of the detective form, Smith says, "Its
key elements are mystery, foreshadowing, memory,

questioning, and discovery." The critic illustrates how each of these elements are found
within *Winter in the Blood.*

Thackeray, William W. "'Crying for Pity' in
    Winter in the Blood." *MELUS,* 7:1 (Spring
    1980), 61-78.
Thackeray argues that in this century the Gros
Ventre tribe is more closely aligned with the
Arapaho Nation than with the Blackfeet Nation.
The critic suggests that an understanding of Gros
Ventre/Arapaho culture can greatly facilitate
one's understanding of Welch's novel. Thackeray
points out, for example, that at 32 years of age,
the crucial tests for mature manhood began for
the Gros Ventre/Arapaho male. The critic states
that the young man had to pass through eight
stages to attain manhood. Thackeray traces how
the narrator moves through these stages during
the course of the novel, but points out that the
protagonist is stalled for a long while at the
second stage, "'crying for pity' or debasing
oneself, occasionally torturing oneself, so that
God will look upon one with pity."

Velie, Alan R. "*Winter in the Blood* as Comic
    Novel." *American Indian Quarterly,* 4
    (1978), 141-47.
Velie argues that Indian novels are almost always
misread as protest novels. The critic stresses
that *Winter in the Blood* is a "comic novel" and
defines the term: "a fiction which contains a
liberal amount of humor--or, to put it most con-
cisely, a funny book." Much more of the author's
article is devoted to an analysis of the comic
novel than to an analysis of Welch's work. Velie
differs from several other critics by viewing the
funeral scene as purely comical: "Quite clearly
he is presenting the situation comically so that
it will amuse the reader."

Velie, Alan R. "*Winter in the Blood*: Welch
    and the Comic Novel." *Four American Indian*

> *Literary Masters*, Norman: University of
> Oklahoma Press, 1982. (Although similar to
> Velie's essay *"Winter in the Blood* as Comic
> Novel." *American Indian Quarterly*, 3:1
> (1978), 141-47, this chapter has numerous
> textural differences.)

Velie begins by defining the term, "comic
novel." The critic argues that tone and characterization, not the endings of novels, give the
basis for differentiation between comic and non-
comic novels. The critic traces the linking of
scenes, climactic and anticlimactic, in the
novel.

> Wilson, Norma. "Outlook for Survival."
> *Denver Quarterly*, 14 (Winter 1980), 22-30.

Wilson traces the use of the American Indian oral
tradition in modern Native American literature.
Although the critic deals primarily with Leslie
Silko's poetry and novel, *Ceremony*, she also
alludes to Welch's *Winter in the Blood*. Wilson
states that "veterans of World War II are central
characters in *House Made of Dawn*, and *Winter in
the Blood*, as well as *Ceremony*. A major dif-
ference between *Ceremony* and the other two novels
is that Tayo's progression back to health is more
complete than that of Abel and the unnamed veteran in *Winter in the Blood*."

Criticism of *The Death of Jim Loney*

> Allen, Paula Gunn. "A Stranger in My Own
> Life: Alienation in American Indian Prose
> and Poetry." *MELUS*, 7 (Summer 1980), 3-
> 19.

Allen suggests that a preoccupation with the
process of alienation is central to contemporary
American Indian writing. In a discussion of such
writers as Welch, Leslie Silko, and N. Scott
Momaday, Allen finds that alienation is characteristic of the life of the Indian "half or mixed
blood." She states that Loney "does not come to
self-realization and the healing that accompanies

it so gently." Of *The Death of Jim Loney* she
states, "This most brutal and honest of the
novels written about alienated mixed blood
Indians portrays the exact process of alienation
which offers no possibility of relief."

Lewis, Robert, "James Welch's *The Death of Jim
    Loney.*" *Studies in American Indian
    Literatures*, 5:3 (1981).
Lewis first notes parallels between Welch's two
novels and then explains how the novels vary.
The critic spends some time comparing the points
of view in the two works and moves into an
analysis of the "roving narration" found in *The
Death of Jim Loney*. Lewis notes that this narration reveals that characters react both nega-
tively and positively to Loney without knowing
why they respond the way they do. The critic
finally analyzes the function of the Biblical
quote which begins the work and argues that the
action of the novel is a turning from man to God,
"but Loney has no God to turn to to save him."

Lincoln, Kenneth. *Native American Renaissance.*
    Berkeley, CA: University of California
    Press, 1983, 164-173.
Lincoln devotes several pages of his book to a
discussion of *The Death of Jim Loney*. The critic
analyzes the narrator's name which he sees as a
play on nicknaming an Indian "The Lone Ranger."
The critic traces the way the details of small
town life flesh out the novel but argues that the
characters are "neither low enough for tragic
depth nor high enough for insight." Lincoln
observes that there is little Blackfeet ethnology
in the novel and states that Welch seems "to
write an American 'breed's' novel." The critic
concludes that "the novel comes across more as
ideas than execution."

Owens, Louis. "The Absurd Indian: Humor in the
    Novels of James Welch." *The Language of
    Humor the Humor of Language.* (Proceedings

of the 1982 WHIM Conference). Edited by Don
L. Nilsen; Co-editor, Alleen Pace Nilsen.
1983, 140-143.
In this discussion of *Winter in the Blood* and *The
Death of Jim Loney*, Owens examines comic elements
in both novels. This critic states that Welch
makes use of surrealism and black humor to depict
the absurdity of contemporary Indian existence,
an absurdity which stems from Indians' lack of
harmony with their heritage and history. Owens
examines comic scenes in both of Welch's novels
and argues that the works protest the conditions
of modern Indian life: "They protest the role of
the Indian as the victim of absurd if sometimes
comical chance on a 'great earth of stalking
white men.'"

Sands, Kathleen M. *"The Death of Jim Loney*:
    Indian or Not?" *S.A.I.L.*, 5:3-4 (1981).
The critic argues that Welch's second novel
expands the ground upon which most Indian fiction
rests. Sands initially traces the common elements which one usually finds in a work of Indian
literature--influence of oral tradition, concern
with landscape, and collapse of sequential time--
and illustrates how Welch makes little or no use
of these factors. She argues that Welch depends
in his novel on elements of tradition "supported
by [a] controlled and rather delicate infusion of
qualities associated with Indian literature."
Although acknowledging the strains of alienation
throughout the work, Sands does not see *The Death
of Jim Loney* as a novel of emptiness or despair.

Thackeray, William W. *"The Death of Jim Loney*
    As a Half-Breed's Tragedy." *Studies in
    American Indian Literatures*, 5:3 (1981).
The critic finds the fact that Welch has written
about self-induced death "not only surprising,
[but] disconcerting." Thackeray questions
whether the novel is truly a tragedy and concludes that "Loney's choice of the White world is
his tragic flaw." The critic feels that Loney

represents the dilemma which every Indian male
faces: "Either abandon Indian heritage and try
to make it in the White world, thus to be cut off
from the life-granting Indian culture, or give up
one's White-world identity hoping to find oneself
somewhere in Indian traditions."

Reviews of *Winter in the Blood*

America. Vol. 132, April 11, 1976, 306.
American Indian Quarterly. Vol. 1, no. 3,
    Autumn 1974, 201-202.
American West. Vol. 16, May 1979, 48.
Atlantic Monthly. January 1976, 88.
Best Sellers. Vol. 34, January 15, 1975, 473.
Critique. Vol. 20, August 1978, 93.
Critique. Vol. 40, April 1980, 233.
Hudson Review. Summer 1976, 309.
Library Journal. Vol. 99, December 1, 1974,
    3148.
New Letters. Vol. 41, no. 3, March 1975, 110-
    111.
New Republic. Vol. 171, December 14, 1974,
    26.
New York Times. October 3, 1974, 49.
New York Times Book Review. November 10,
    1974, 1.
New York Times Review of Books. Vol. 21,
    December 12, 1974, 18.
New York Times book Review. April 12, 1981,
    43.
New Republic. Vol. 171, December 14, 1974,
    26.
New Yorker. Vol. 50, December 23, 1974, 84.
Newsweek. Vol. 84, November 11, 1974, 119.
Thoreau Journal Quarterly. Vol. 9, no. 1,
    January 1977, 26-28.
Virginia Quarterly Review. Vol. 51, 1975,
    CLII.

Reviews of *The Death of Jim Loney*

Antioch. Vol. 38, Summer 1980, 386-387.
Atlantic Monthly. Vol. 244, October 1979,
    108.
Best Sellers. Vol. 39, December 1979, 327.
Booklist. Vol. 76, October 15, 1979, 334.
Iowa Review. Vol. 10, no. 4, 1979, 110-111.
Kirkus Review. Vol. 47, July 1, 1979, 762.
Library Journal. Vol. 104, September 1979,
    214.
London Times Literary Supplement. May 2,
    1980, 560.
Nation. Vol. 229, November 24, 1979, 538.
New Statesman. Vol. 99, May 2, 1980, 682.
New Yorker. November 4, 1979, 14.
New York Times Book Review. November 4, 1979,
    14.
New York Times Book Review. November 24,
    1979, 25.
New York Times Book Review. April 12, 1981,
    43.
Publisher's Weekly. Vol. 216, July 23, 1979,
    155.
Saturday Review. Vol. 6, November 10, 1979,
    54.
Times Literary Supplement. May 2, 1980, 500.
Western American Literature. Vol. 15, no. 3,
    1980, 219-220.
World Literature Today. Vol. 54, Summer 1980,
    473.

Biographical Sources

American Indian II. Ed. by John R. Milton.
    Vermillion, S.D.: University of South
    Dakota Press, 1971.
Contemporary Literary Criticism. Detroit: Gale
    Research Co., 1976.
Contemporary Poets. 2nd Edition. Ed. by James
    Vinson and D.L. Kirpatrick. New York: St.
    Martin's Press, 1970.

A Directory of American Poets. New York: Poets and Writers, Inc., 1975.

Los Angeles Times. March 30, 1983.

Modern Poetry of Western America. Ed. by Clinton F. Larson & William Stafford. Provo, Utah: Brigham Young University Press, 1975.

New York Times Magazine. December 27, 1981.

Saturday Review World. December 14, 1974.

Voices From Wah'Kon-tah. Ed. by Robert K. Dodge & Joseph B. McCullough. New York: International Publishers, 1974.